Avatar-Philosophy (and -Religion)

or

FAITHEISM

Edmond Wright

SOCIETAS
essays in political
& cultural criticism

imprint-academic.com

Published in the UK by Societas
Imprint Academic, PO Box 200, Exeter EX5 5YX, UK

Published in the USA by Societas
Imprint Academic, Philosophy Documentation Center
PO Box 7147, Charlottesville, VA 22906-7147, USA

ISBN 9781845402341

A CIP catalogue record for this book is available from the
British Library and US Library of Congress

To Samuel, Daniel, Thomas and Joel

'Nothing does us as much good as a *fool's cap*.'

Friedrich Nietzsche,
The Gay Science, Book II, section 107

'The imagination is the secret and marrow of civilization.
It is the very eye of faith.'

Henry Ward Beecher,
Proverbs from Plymouth Pulpit, 1887

Contents

Introduction

So you have seen *Avatar*. Are you someone for whom all this talk of 'Gaia', here the Na'vi 'Eywa', is New-Age nonsense? And are you someone, like the atheist Richard Dawkins, for whom all this talk of divine beings, in trees or out of them, is primitive-savage nonsense? Or, from the other side, are you the Vatican solemnly warning against the film because it encourages pantheism, the notion of God identical with the universe? Or are you an orthodox Hindu protesting against this take-over of their sacred concept? Or are you the Chinese government—who have censored 'Avatar' for mass showing (ordering the showing of a life of Confucius instead)—for they are reading 'Uighur' or 'Tibetan' or 'Falun Gong' into the Na'vi—or 'Tamil' for the Sri Lankan government,—or the 'Yanomami tribe' for the Brazilian rain-forest loggers (Who's burned the tree?)—or are you a redneck from Tennessee seeing the tribe as blatantly native-American-Indian or African-American, and James Cameron as much as a 'Na'vi-lover' as his 'Jake Sully'? —perhaps a redneck already enraged by the film *District 9*, which also has in Koobus Venter a sadistic soldier like *Avatar*'s Colonel Quaritch, and its 'prawn-lover', Wikus van der Merwe—And what is more remarkable, in the last shot of the film we see that Wikus has become an avatar himself, transformed into as convincing a 'prawn' as Jake is a Na'vi. Then there is Neo in *The Matrix* (1999) who can appear in a virtual body in the digital world while he lies supine in a control room on an underground vessel. In the Bruce Willis film *Surrogates* (2009), all outside activity, as supposedly in the web game *Second Life*, is carried on through surrogate robots. We have had an avatar not so long ago on British TV screens, in the popular series *Life on Mars* (2006–7), in which it seems that a policeman, Sam Tyler, his head injured in an accident, lies helpless, like Neo and Jake Sully, this time in a hospital in 2006, while he experiences another life back in 1973, where he too meets a violent authority-figure, this time a police chief inspector, Gene Hunt. James Cameron's other science fiction venture, *The Terminator*, can be said to have an avatar character, for the cyborg, though not monitored moment by moment by his controllers, has had an identity imprinted in his circuits from elsewhere, one defined by a single purpose. Further back in time, there is Wim Wenders' *Wings of Desire* of 1987, a story of an angel upon Earth in a human body, and, by contrast, *The Exorcist* (1973), in which an innocent child becomes possessed by the Devil. In 1973 there was Rainer Fassbinder's *World on a Wire*, which anticipates *The Matrix* by 32 years. *The Exorcist* is matched by *The Invasion of the Body-Snatchers* (1956), with its own forebears in Gothic literature, the tales of *Doppelgängers* (Stevenson's *The Strange Case of Dr. Jekyll and Mr. Hyde*, Poe's *William Wilson*), and of vampires (Sheridan Le Fanu's *Carmilla*, Bram Stoker's *Dracula*, and most recently, *Buffy the Vampire Slayer*), again stories of corruption of the innocent. Is this not something too much of coincidence?

And then there is the question of the fairy-story denouement, a 'Here comes the cavalry to the rescue!' (or Tolkien's eagles or C.S. Lewis's 'Aslan') in the form of bullet-proof fantasy-dinosaurs, 'titanotheres', bulldozing the Marines down. Is this a myth we should be serving up to our children in this world of mad fundamentalists? Isn't it positively seditious in a world with Wootton Bassett in it? Better be with Commander James T. Kirk who at the last minute would have ordered Scottie 'to beam the Marines up'.

One can't be content with those kneejerk reactions above. There is a way of looking at the film that doesn't take up any of those attitudes, one that doesn't get trapped into fundamentalist-religious fixations on the one hand or Dawkinsian derision on the other. One aspect of the film that can't be ignored is its spectacular fantasy world with its lithe and beautiful people — as well as the grim pterodactyl-helicopters and the ankylosaurus-air-tanks of Colonel Quaritch. The film excites wonder at its mythical beauty and grotesquerie in equal measure as myths have always done. But what has all this to do with questions of political and religious faith?

One

Just what is an Avatar?

The Hindus do have a right to claim the first use of the word. 'Avatar' as a word derives from the Sanskrit 'ava', *down*, and 'tarati', *he crosses over*. It is used of the highest god, Vishnu, who temporarily takes over a human body on earth, to create a godlike being, Krishna, who performs tasks on his behalf; he has come *down* and *crossed over* into the sublunary realm. It is obviously what we would call an 'incarnation', literally *in the flesh*, because we note the match with 'God the Father' who sent his son Christ to carry out his mission in the lower world. What is central to the meaning is the notion of the controller remaining in the upper world and the body in the lower carrying out his desired actions at one remove. Incarnation is a topic to which we shall return.

This relationship of control at one remove has in our time been humbly reproduced on various occasions as an outcome of our new-found electronic wizardry. Steve Moulton, a Philco engineer in the US, describes the strange experience he had when he tried on a 'TV-hood' over his eyes, the input to the screen of which came from a camera at the top of a building he was in (he was on the ground floor).

The camera was so arranged that it moved from right to left, scanning the landscape around, exactly in accordance with the sideways movements of his head. A weird effect was produced by this matching of movement, which Moulton called 'creepy': he could not escape having the sensation of *being up in the tower in the position of the camera looking around at the landscape*. It was an avatar-experience at a minimal level (for the details, see Daniel Dennett, 1983, 24–1).

In experiments at University College, London, and the Catalan Institute of Research and Advanced Studies, Mel Slater, an investigator in this field, has been testing the effect of wearing virtual reality headsets.[1] He has been able to show that men who wore virtual reality headsets that gave them the impression that they were occupying a female body were unable, while wearing them, to shake off the perceptual impression that they had such a body. The impression, of course, stopped as soon as the headsets were removed.

My philosophy tutor at Oxford, Gareth Evans, was also intrigued by the idea of experience at one remove. In his book *The Varieties of Reference* (Evans, 1982, 166–70), he imagines, specifically in order to explore the notion of reference to spatial position, a naval operative inside a ship who is in control of a submarine device that is exploring the sea-bed. He compares him to 'the experienced driver of a mechanical excavator', who, I am sure you can recognize already, is another, if partial, avatar (the driver is still using his own eyes). The naval operative, however, is not using his eyes underwater: he has an indirect access to the scene

---

[1]   *The Guardian*, 12/05/2010; originally in the web journal *PLoS One*, URL: http://www.plosone.org/article/info:doi/10.1371/journal. pone.0010564

on the sea-bed by means of a television camera. The submarine 'is equipped with limbs, excavators, etc., and a means of propulsion remotely controllable by the subject' (p. 166). He suggests that, if the operative were to be 'insulated from the sounds, smells, sights and so on around him', that is, in the ship, he could 'play' at being where the submarine is. Evans is still disinclined to allow him to conceive of his 'here' as being on the sea-bed, but, with our having read Dennett's account, we would allow him to think of two *here's* — on the sea-bed and in the ship, depending on how he is *playing*, that is, with consideration for what is relevant in the context of speech to someone else. Evans goes on to say that the operative might even think to himself 'I'll pick up that rock' — and that thought turns him into a minimal avatar. If you have lost something down a crevice, and you poke around with a stick, you will have the 'play' sensation of feeling with the end of the stick.

I myself, as a philosopher of mind, took the scenario one stage further, one that brings the situation nearer to the human one. I envisaged a set-up in which there were *two* operatives, each equipped with his own elaborate device, and they were having to discuss with each other over the phone — as they were not together — precisely what it was they were dealing with. I imagined them as bomb-disposers, which made it essential that, in sending their devices out to an unfamiliar bomb (a safe distance away), they could inspect it and discuss the details of what it was they were 'seeing' as they attempted to dismantle it.[2] The Dennett Effect I took to be working for both of them, but, as you can readily understand, they kept being faced with problems of identifying exactly what it was they were deal-

[2]   For the full account see Wright, 2005, Chapter 3, part 6.

ing with. I gave a sample of a possible conversation, and it becomes plain that both are quite happy to talk as if they are present at the bomb, and one's corrections of the other — since he has a different perspective on what is going on — prove useful. They are, in fact, playing a dangerous guessing-game with the real world that lies in front of the cameras, and their individual guesses have to be subject to mutual correction if they are to be successful. As part of my larger argument, I maintain that this gets close to the actual process in human language, which I here shall claim to be a sort of double-avatar state of affairs.

Since they are both uncertain, they have to trust each other about what they are actually referring to, and this is where *faith* enters the picture. It is plain that both of them are working on the assumption that their further aims are the same. Faith will be our concern over the next few pages, but you must allow an atheist to lead you by a roundabout way through the wood, one that leads right back past Krishna and Christ to an explanation of how the myth of avatarhood has relevance for us at this time in history.

Two

So what is Faith?

In their best-selling books, what the atheists Richard Dawkins, Christopher Hitchens, Daniel Dennett, and Michel Onfray neglect, for all their palpable (and entertaining) hits on organized religion, is what faith is when it is divested of the trappings of belief in the divine. They have been fazed by the way organized religion has monopolized the word — and, consequently, and unwisely, they neglect *the human virtue itself*. Faith for Dawkins is no virtue at all — it is even 'pernicious' to teach it as one (Dawkins, 2006, 247); Hitchens equates it with blind belief (Hitchens, 2007, 254-9); similarly for Dennett, quoting Mark Twain, faith is a 'meme' that encourages you 'to believe what you know ain't so' (Dennett, 2006, 321); for Onfray, all entertaining of myth, such as a vision of an after-life, is 'a really deadly sin' (Onfray, 2007, 217). They all confine faith to the stories the religious tell about how life must be viewed. You will find no examination by the authors above of what faith could possibly be when not hidden inside the array of tales paraded for us as revealed truth in the holy books, whether it is faith in the Resurrection of the Body, or Padre Pio's levitation, or Elijah's chariot ride to Heaven, or Ganesha's race with Kartikay, or Mohammed's splitting of the moon, or whatever. All four of our atheists, of course, would be quick to say that these are on a par with Santa Claus getting round to all those chimneys on Christmas Eve, and they would be partly right — and partly wrong — as we shall see.

But — and this is a real puzzle — why do Dawkins and the rest take this definition of faith for gospel, accepting that it can only be defined as the believers define it, that faith as a concept is not worth analyzsing outside how the Pope and the Archbishop of Canterbury and the Chief Rabbi and Tony Blair and the ayatollahs see it? British politicians of all parties speak of 'faith schools'. Isn't this extraordinary, that opponents so at odds should agree on the term at the core of the argument?

For what is faith? Ironically, if the old-religious read something of their own theologians of the past, they might come across a recurring theme, that faith was precisely *not* to be characterized as certain conviction. There it is, even in the New Testament (Mark, 9:24) — 'Lord, I believe — help Thou mine unbelief.' What this brings to the surface is the truth that risk attends all faith — risk. When you trust some-one else, as you always do when you believe you are speaking to them truthfully, what you cannot be sure of is that they are understanding the words as you do. Both speaker and hearer have to behave *as if* they do, but that constitutes an act of trust in itself, one that we need to speak at all, not a guarantee of certainty. That each of us sees differently, hears differently — and so on through the senses — cannot be denied. Furthermore, since we all learned our words a dif-ferent way, different memories attend them — proved by the psycholinguist Ragnar Rommetveit, who has been able to show that people use very different criteria for identifying what they call the 'same' thing (Rommetveit, 1974, Ch. 4). George Steiner has put it thus: that we each speak an 'idiolect' of our common language (Steiner, 1998, 47). No wonder the two bomb-disposers had to proceed cautiously. And this is at the core of language, the very thing that makes us human.

So if you open that door of apparent certainty, what lies behind it is not at first sight reassuring: what if the sentence you are 'sharing' turns out tomorrow to have dire consequences for you that were not foreseen by you but were innocently taken for granted by your partner in dialogue? However, in some circumstances, all you may have to do to put things right is shrug your shoulders and laugh and accept some minor sacrifice, a comic way out—and your partner may even pre-empt you in this. But what if the sacrifice is far beyond expectations, with a tragic outcome inescapable? Then the power and commitment of your love for the other and theirs for you will enter the sacrificial resolution. You will have 'to love your enemy' in a way never envisaged. And is this not what all the great stories and plays are about, from *King Lear* to *Great Expectations*?

Three

The Game of Language

It is plain that a proper faith has to behave *as if* it is in a myth, a profound one, namely, that one means what one says (when one can't perfectly do so), that one is sincere (when it may turn out that, in your friend's staunch opinion, you are being treacherous) — to put it plainly, that 'your word' that you had 'given' can be relied on to mean something you didn't, that you can in your own eyes be wholly 'faithful', that you are convinced of speaking 'the truth' when your view of 'faithfulness' and 'truth' may not survive time's joke at your expense. There may come a demand for a love 'that passeth' all your earlier 'understanding'. So conviction doesn't enter into it.[1]

It is just like an ordinary game: what you saw in the state of the chess pieces was not what your opponent saw — which might be to your advantage or your disadvantage. Wittgenstein said that there was only a 'family resemblance' across games of different kinds; in this he was mistaken (Wittgenstein, 1967, 31e–32e). All games, even Patience games and the 'bouncing of a ball against a wall', that Wittgenstein mentions, are won by surprising re-interpretations of what appear to be challenges, and so often it is

---

[1]   For further on the 'As If', see Vaihinger, 1924.

a matter of seeing an attendant weakness in that challenge, as when a judo player uses the very momentum of the opponent's attack to unbalance him. What kinds of play gain the applause in tennis? — Surely when one player's shot has the character of a decisive win, say, a shot from the net which drives the ball down and across, but the opponent instantaneously realizes that a ball in just that very direction and with just that force can be turned into an unreachable lob to the back of the court. The language-game is no exception: it is all to do with the changing of interpretations of what our senses present to us. Every informative statement is a hopeful attempt at an update of the other, and that is attended with risk. The means by which we update another is by providing him or her with a clue or clues that changes the context for the 'item' under consideration; sometimes the hearer is quick to find clues to plausible contexts of their own, as of the child who thought a Sousa march was called 'Tarzan Strikes Forever' — no doubt the heroic character of the music was the clue. Take the wrong clue as relevant and you precipitate the danger: the real may trip you up.[2]

We are tempted — on the surface — to get weightily complacent about the real. In our little parochial corner of space-time, we have found that the real seems to tolerate a lot of the words we use; page upon page of the dictionary seems just in order as it is, seemingly apt for our human purposes. Our everyday experience goes on apparently confirming so much of our 'knowledge'. Nice to go on assuming that nothing outside or inside us will give us a surprise — though, notice, we don't complain about pleasant surprises, even though they upset our *assumptions* just

---

[2]   For how language began with the provision of such a clue, see Wright, 2009.

as much as unpleasant ones! — just as in a game, in chess, for example, have you not sometimes experienced surprised relief when some move you thought was a mistake turned out to be an ingenious challenge for your opponent?

Nevertheless, every statement we make is uttered in hope that 'all shall be well' — except for those of the liars, but they fall under the same analysis for lies may be valuable in spite of their utterers. But, since there is no denying that the hoped-for 'communion' of all aims can never be brought about, heaven is only a poetic metaphor for that non-existent goal. It is where the gods of religions reign 'omniscient' where all words are lodged with their eternal referents in the blissful marriage of meaning and real. Incidentally, it has never been pointed out that in that final state of universal heavenly knowledge, with everyone omniscient, no one would need to talk to anyone else; persons would not be concerned to be talking at all if they had the impossibly perfect agreement. As Wilhelm Dilthey pointed out, 'Interpretation would be impossible if the life-expressions were totally alien. It would be unnecessary if there were nothing strange about them' (Dilthey, 1913–67, Vol. 7, 225), that is, we could not talk if we had nothing in common and we would not need to talk if we totally agreed on everything.

Hence, if faith is all a myth, holding to it has to be far more courageous than was ever thought, for there is no such final total identification of word and entity, no bodily immortality to compensate for sacrifice (nor no transcendent hell to punish a failure to accept it). Yet — and this is the paradox of play in the language game — we have to behave to each other *as if* the final happy outcome was guaranteed. The 'cavalry to the rescue', the fantasy dinosaurs chasing the oppressors away, are merely poetic symbols of an impossible hope. For the truth is that we ought to create such fantasies of a final joy as a commitment, not to such a joy, but to a hope that, whatever unforeseen complications occur in the future, we will, through sacrifice, strive to help our partner in the dialogue. Best to copy the persona who speaks one of Thomas Hardy's poems:

> And some day hence, toward paradise
> And all its blest, if such there be,
> I will lift up glad, afar-off eyes
> Though it contain no place for me.

To turn old-philosophical for a moment. If you have asked 'Where is the horse?' of a horse we are acquainted with, and I say 'The horse you wanted is outside', we begin our playing of a little game with an initial stage in which 'The horse' means exactly the same for both of us. It seems to fall in with Plato's view of the matter, that there was an ideal 'Form' of the Horse, uncontaminated with the reality of actual horses, by which we are able to use our word in common. It meant the 'whatness' of the Horse, as James Joyce's Stephen Dedalus put it (Joyce, 1947, 174), because we have picked out by means of it an objective 'What' from the changing flux of the 'That'.[3] Plato was very keen to stress that a Form was 'changeless'. Better to see that 'changelessness' as an illusion created by our very faith in each other, and that, hence, 'the Good', the 'happy outcome for every*body*', cannot be depended upon at all as a transcendent reality. 'The horse outside' might be an unrideable hack, but, if that 'fact' was outside my knowing, perhaps outside everyone's, it is not straightforward to blame me, automatically call me 'insincere', for my 'what' was not the same as yours and I didn't know.

[3]   See Josiah Royce on the distinction between the 'What' and the 'That': Royce, 1976 [1899], I, 49-52.

Four

The Mutually Imagined Singularity

The old-religious want faith to deliver heaven after all, even though all 'reason' is against it; this, by the way, is part of what they are saying when *they* say, 'Faith isn't certain.' Just a word on why they are so misled. It concerns what their 'faith' focuses upon. The real — all existence — is indeed a frightening place (both outside and inside us). When the old-religious enter into the 'as if' of language, namely, that we all mean exactly the same by our words, guaranteed by the dictionary and, initially, by 'the Good' or 'God', they want to be sure that when they refer to something, there is only *one* 'true' thing they are referring to. That is hardly surprising, since we could not co-ordinate our actually differing takes on the real at all unless, like the bomb-disposers, we did behave *as if* there were perfectly singular things before us all. The two engaged in language have to begin with the mutual assumption that they have picked out exactly the same entity from the Real, same in virtually a timeless sense, in that they are both taking for granted that there is one entity that pre-exists their attempts to single 'it' out, and that, whatever criteria they each may be using, 'it' is there as an unchanging 'referent' awaiting the joint 'reference'. After all, if they did not take singularity for granted, they would not even be able to get a rough purchase on the real; their differing perspectives could not be drawn into the necessary partial overlap that allows the correction which is the aim of the statement to go through. They would be talking past each other. To avoid that is what one of Plato's 'Forms', *used just as a provisional tool*, is for. Once the imaginary 'common' focus has been established, the speaker can introduce a clue which transforms the meaning, just as in a joke.

To illustrate with a simple example of why a mutual pretence of common single reference is needed and why it does not actually exist. To get the joke-like absurdity clear: in the following scenario Speaker A knows that her view of a region of the real is different from that of Hearer B, yet both have to begin the statement with the assumption that they are talking about a single definable entity, knowable in the same way to both of them. They end up acknowledging that 'it' was not singular. Listen to this interchange. It takes place between two birdwatchers who are busily counting birds:

A: That bird you just counted.
B: Well, what about it?
A: It was two-and-a-bit leaves.

The advantage of two heads being better than one is well demonstrated by this little interchange. What was taken to be a single entity at the start ended up by being seen later as 'two-and-a-bit'. A could not have brought B's attention to the part of the real she was concerned about unless they had both behaved as if there were a singular referent, 'the bird', in front of them. The last line constitutes the transforming clue. Compare a simple joke: 'As guests go, you wish he would' (Anon.). Where the last four words transform the meaning of 'go' from the originally assumed *turn out to be* to *leave* (see Wright, 2005, opening chapter).

Worthwhile here examining what is meant by the simple pronoun 'it' in its two appearances in the dialogue, and then you will see how *the game is played*. The structure is the same as that tennis shot I described, and is the same in *all* attempts at informative statements. One can compare this mutual, hopeful projection of logical singularity to a catalyst in a chemical combination: it enables the process to go through, but it itself is unchanged by that process — so here for the birdwatchers, the idea of singularity moved easily on to help in the rearrangement of our purchase on the real — 'one' bird as the 'common' focus becoming 'two-and-a-bit' leaves as the 'common' focus. What is paradoxical is that we do want to maintain agreement with our partner in speech, and yet to extend our understanding to the other we have virtually 'to deceive' him or her.

But we can never count in exactly the same way. William Wordsworth has a nice way of making this point. In a poem, 'We are seven' in his *Lyrical Ballads*, he has a grown-up asking a little girl how many children there are in her family. She answers 'Seven', but it transpires that she is counting in 'the two of us that in the churchyard lie'. He tries to correct her, but finds that it 'is throwing words away'. Wordsworth was making an underlying criticism of the Enlightenment philosopher William Godwin, for whom rationality was the prime ethical guide.

The social theorist Alfred Schutz called this mutual projection by partners in language of there initially being a singular referent to work with in this move in the language game a 'reciprocity of perspectives', and 'the idealization of the interchangeability of the standpoints', the taking for granted that, if I were in your shoes, your standpoint would seem to be the same as mine, you and I seeing 'things' with the same typicality (Schutz, 1962, 11–12). My own way of describing this trick by which we get a rough mutual grasp on the Real has been to say 'It is by a PRETENCE of *complete* success that we *partially* capture THE REAL' (Wright, 1978, 538). The 'guest' joke worked on the same principle, the undercutting of an *assumed* agreement. This was necessary because the motivation of any statement is a desire to update the other about some challenge in the real, some unexpected disharmony of understanding, whether slight or urgent in its implications.

The old-religious take a further step: ready to admit that we have all got different perspectives on the real, they go on to the belief that, when we refer in a statement in speech, there is ONE thing *already there* to be referred to. The real is there all right, netted temporarily in the rough focus of our converging perspectives. Nevertheless, there is no proof that at the core of that 'rough focus' is *a logically pure singularity with precisely the same criteria of definition for everyone.* Around this they can project the aura of certainty which can thus enhance all 'things', all 'persons' and all 'selves'. One can say that they are taking literally the pragmatic mutual hypothesis we all have to employ if we are to talk at all.[1]

A key question for the old-religious, indeed anyone who is concerned to hold on to the notion of a given objectivity, is to ask them 'What precisely is the difference between behaving *as if* there is one logically singular entity before us both and there actually being one?' No difference can be

---

[1]   For a lucid explanation of how we are tempted to think mistakenly that all of the real can be carved out into given things and persons without residue see the first chapter of Stuart Hampshire's *Thought and Action*, 1970, 11–89.

detected in our behaviour: first, because the process of mutual correction can continue for ever without a final arrival at a purely determinate result; second, since our perspectives remain stubbornly different, we can never lock our understandings into perfect agreement, even should a singular entity really exist, so an ontological belief in it is quite unnecessary; third, any immediate agreement is made relative to our judgements of what is relevant to our purposes in what we are sensing, and, because of the limitations of our perceptual judgements, there is never a guarantee that, at a later time, what one person (A) considers to be relevant will not emerge as a surprise to the other (B), but was innocently taken for granted by A at the earlier time but never mentioned because it entirely ignored as utterly negligible. So, in answer to the question posed at the beginning of this paragraph, the only difference is the acceptance that, since the singularity of the entity is beyond any mutual ascertaining, one has to be prepared for the challenge of *granting* something in the future never envisaged (perhaps the number of entities involved, perhaps the criteria of identity, perhaps the very existence of what was 'identified' at the earlier time). This challenge of, for you, the unexpected dissolution of the former 'objectivity' of which you were convinced, may bring the prospect of the necessity of a painful renunciation of some cherished purpose. The belief in singularity takes no account of this ethical problem. Equally, a completely unexpected *furthering of one's purposes* can emerge at the later time, which, as can be readily conceded, is no proof of singularity either.

So which is the ethically preferable stance? — to accept that a comic or tragic outcome is possible for you with its consequent implication of the necessity of sacrifice without divine reward, or to disguise this result from yourself with a belief that your own judgement of 'objectivity' and 'truth' was based on a given singularity in the real? The former demands a proper faith, one that accepts an ever-present risk: the latter offers a mirage of comforting certainty, one dressed up in terms like 'truth', 'sincerity', 'realism' and 'objectivity'. That supposedly independent truth has a tendency to turn into the illusion of an apparently undeniable proof to sustain the rigid conviction, within which any 'behaving *as if* can thus be rejected as relativist pretence. Anyone taking this view forgets Touchstone's dictum: 'Much virtue in "if"' (Shakespeare, *As You Like It*, V, iv, 105). Should the objectivist concede that our judgements are endlessly corrigible, then he or she has given up the claim that in the real a singular entity awaits a final, mutually agreed definition, for the only purpose served by that ideal is the practical one of getting a rough co-ordination of our differing perspectives on the region of the real that seems to concern us all.

Further still, some of the old-religious believe that God has arranged these singular things all in logically perfect order, a *divine system* we may not have got through to yet, but hovers there just out of reach beyond the vagaries and illusions of this world as the 'true' foundation of our speech. In their view, the 'reality' of things behind the 'appearance' has got to be *countable and nameable*; it has to be a system of countable things capturable by our words. That is their 'faith', for, having no proof of this hidden order, they cling on to countability being part of real existence. God is a mathematician, they say. Even God himself, in their 'faith', is taken to be objectively real, — indeed, He is the only entity that really deserves the name 'The One' (Plotinus, 1934 [ca.

253], 160-3), although, as they are quick to add, it cannot be proved, nor should the attempt to prove it be made. However, to summarize, the idea that 'true singularity' is an illusion is created by four aspects of this situation:

1) the need *to assume singularity as the means by which a rough coincidence of the differing perspectives of partners in dialogue is achieved*; and

2) the underlying need *to have faith in each other precisely because we are both only ASSUMING that singularity*, which has the implication that agreement may only be partial in significant respects *without our mutually being aware of it*;

3) because we would rather believe that we *have* captured the real successfully, and, *because to doubt it suggests obscurely that we mistrust our partner in dialogue*, we are tempted into forgetting our undeniable differences in the illusion of a logically singular thing, and into not noticing that we are mutually imagining it — and *have to* mutually imagine it, otherwise we would not be able to talk;

4) a perfect happiness is imagined as the final goal of all our motivation, and so the perfect oneness of all our knowings is taken as a guarantee of that, the basis of all 'transcendence'. A strange consequence is that singularity, not only is never questioned, but is handled as if it had no connection with our fears and desires, the unconscious effect being to keep the fears out of view. It becomes an *impersonal, even eternal* fact, nothing to do with our personal wishes and emotions in this world of time, which it would seem bad form to bring to mutual salience.

The fourth aspect also shows itself in the arguments of some philosophers, for example, Gilbert Harman, for whom, if we are all looking at a tree, even if we all have our differing perspectives, they are still perspectives upon 'it'. What we see can only be 'features of the presented tree', Harman,

1990, 38–9). This conviction of there being only one object provides a block against the disturbing thought that there is no divine system, no ultimately safe and secure set of namings. You can see how this conviction of order existing *now* is taken for a guarantee of the final emergence of the match of human word to that universal order, a kind of proof of its possibility. You can thus see why many people are resistant to rejecting the notion of secure objectivity, for the reason is that they unconsciously sense that it appears to be a threat to that crowning hope. No wonder some attribute a mystical divinity to a 'given uniqueness' of all entities, particularly the 'soul'. The poet Gerard Manley Hopkins is an example (see his sonnet 'As kingfishers catch fire'

> Each mortal thing does one thing and the same:
> Deals out that being indoors each one dwells.

By contrast, another poet, Wordsworth, was well aware that both minds and the real played a part in 'what' we perceive:

> Of all the mighty world
> Of eye and ear, — *both what they half create,*
> *And what perceive.* [2]

One philosopher, David Wiggins, made the following objection to this concept of the 'Thing': of course there is vagueness in the identification of everything, but where something is vague, *it is vague in the same way for everyone*; 'the object is there to be found' (Wiggins, 2001, 11–12). But this is simply false: a criterion that is vague or entirely irrelevant for me may be highly specific for you. In what I regard as of no account, you may find a key relevance. Our differing perspectives may get very close, but they can never snap into the imagined perfect alignment. But we *have to* imagine

---

[2]   William Wordsworth, 'Lines composed a Few Miles above Tintern Abbey', lines 105–7; my emphasis.

together that 'the object is to be found': that is the measure of our faith.

As a rough analogy to the actual state of affairs as regards what we call 'things', 'persons' and 'selves', I often think of those experiments that photographers are sometimes tempted to make in which transparencies of a hundred faces, say of beautiful women, are carefully superimposed on each other so that none of them fail to make contribution to the final image that is a compound of them all. What results is a curious, slightly fuzzy picture of an idealized face, like that of a Renaissance angel in a holy painting. In a similar way, all our ideas of what any 'referent', though assumed by us all to be an ideal, logically singular entity objectively existing in the real, is only the fuzzy compounding of all our private, and therefore distinct, selections – and yet we are only sensing our own selection, at the same time *taking it for* the ideal.

Of course, when we learned language we all worked on the crude principle that a name corresponded to a singular entity, the principle that the philosopher Gilbert Ryle scoffingly called the 'Fido-"Fido"' theory of reference, that is, believing that each name fitted one thing without any awkward residues (Ryle, 1971, Vol. II). But we don't think in such philosophical terms; it is clearly just a habit that our mode of learning our language has instilled into us. The four reasons given above for accepting the notion of singularity are not consciously held at all; they are just part of a general set of assumptions habitually deemed too obvious to inquire into. That is why any challenge of them seems so bizarre. Objectivity is comfortingly customary; we enjoy the feeling of secure agreement with others that the belief in it affords us; the German sociologist Christian Etzrodt recently reminded me how powerful this was in establishing the prejudice (personal communication).

One can fairly draw their attention of the old-religious to the opening of St. John's Gospel: 'In the beginning was the *Word*'. Notice, in particular, it did not say 'In the beginning was *God* .' On the contrary, the very next statement is 'the Word was God'. So one has to say to them, 'Yes, it is, in an allegorical sense, "God" who guarantees the truth of one's "singular" reference, but "God" is the *human* faith that the partners in dialogue have that their selections from the real match perfectly, while knowing at the same time — both of them — that it is impossible that they should.' No such being as 'God' exists. What does exist is *the mutual faith that ought to ensure that the emergence of some hidden disagreement will be met with the willingness of love to make a sacrifice*.

This is why 'the Good' and 'the True' cannot be identified with any selection from the real that you happen to have made. One insidious temptation is to take one's own selection as 'objective': notice that your selection is certainly *from* the real, but it is easy to forget that someone else's selection, also *from* the real, *cannot match your own*, even though you both have to call it 'the same object' in order to get the needful overlap required for a statement to go through, as the Birdwatchers example shows. It is very difficult for the objectivist philosopher to disentangle his own perspective from the imagined 'public' one. A good example of such a philosopher is Robert Brandom, who is clearly bemused by the fact that 'the thing' in one's own perspective certainly *exists* and is led, like Harman, to identifying it with a 'public' object. His way of putting it is to say that all can be made 'explicit', claiming the existence of an inflexible objective *singular* actuality that is the same for all participants in a dialogue (Brandom, 1994, 20). My response, from years ago, is to say *'What is implicit for each cannot all be explicit for both'* (Wright, 1978, 541). Nor does our own perspective pick out *one* clearly delineated portion of the real, for even within what we are attending to are elements of sensation to which we are giving no significance.

What is the motivation of this unwarranted projection of the 'as if'? It is vital to confront this temptation for it leads to what I regard as the most common and deep-rooted of prejudices. One immediate answer we have seen is to point to the sense of security it gives to believe that the real comes conveniently parceled in John McDowell's 'thus-and-so' entities (McDowell, 1994, 42). But another, less obvious, lies in the third aspect analysed above: it is *de rigueur* not to cast doubt on the reliability of one's partner in dialogue. We are all consciously or otherwise aware that trust is involved in 'true' speech. So to propose that there is a basic uncertainty in the assumed single entity (person, self or object) strikes one as obscurely treacherous, a case of double-dealing. Almost instinctively, one wants to reject the idea. Why 'instinctively'? — (a) first, as insisted upon above, because it seems to challenge the basic trust, and thus seems to amount to an open suspicion of the person to whom you are talking; (b) second, one does not want to doubt the 'objectivity' of our familiar sorting of the real into the mundane world of 'reality', a doubt which seems so bizarre as to be preposterous; and (c) third, one is obscurely aware that, if the two persons engaged in speech did not make this strictly false move — that they were both referring to the 'same' entity — no statement could be made!

But this is not ordinary dialogue: we are here engaged in a philosophical analysis of what goes on in speech, in particular, what the ethical character of that trust should be. As a philosopher, I can be fairly likened to a surgeon operating on an anaesthetized patient, a surgeon who is in the process of lifting a layer of living tissue in order to reveal the anatomy of the human—as will be shown shortly, one can almost say, the anatomy of the soul. It does not at all imply that faith is not imperative in our speech: on the contrary, *it is showing why faith, rather than blind trust, is obligatory.* And why? Because there is an unnoticed element of innocent 'double-dealing' in all informative communication, which renders suspect the blind trust, for you cannot rely on your own understanding of the 'word' as being finally definitive. This is an unavoidable feature of the 'double-avatar' situation, its structure being the same as that of the two Bomb-Disposers. You have to take account of possible differences both in the other's sensing and in the other's understanding, which may demand unexpected sacrifice on your part. Is it not extremely tempting, then, to ignore that deeply disturbing possibility? And the most obvious way of ignoring that is to insist on the singularity of any 'entity' mutually referred to—*a fortiori*, 'persons' and 'selves'.

A further word about blind trust. Blind trust fakes certainty without realizing it. So determined not to face the fear, it regards any suggestion that 'truth', 'the facts', 'objectivity' and the rest are not certain is a symptom of unethical betrayal, a 'relativist' hoax performed by a double-dealer, who cannot be trusted in turn. Alan Sokal is a typical example of those who pour delighted, but ignorant, scorn on those who argue that the objective world where the empirical laws that 'the Enlightenment' has delivered to us hold sway might not be so secure (Sokal, 2010). It does not occur to him to ask why the human term 'law' is, most curiously, used for the projected patterns we have so far found adequate (he might do well to recall that human 'laws' are alterable in democratic assemblies). Faith, on the other hand, moves hand in hand with fear. I would rather keep in mind to what Wordsworth raised the song of thanks and praise:

> But for those obstinate questionings
> Of sense and outward things,
> Fallings from us, vanishings;
> Blank misgivings of a Creature
> Moving about in worlds not realized,
> High instincts before which our mortal Nature
> Did tremble like a guilty thing surprised.[3]

Notice how, in the last two lines here, he cannot refrain from expressing his *fear* of 'moving about in worlds not realized', *which is what we are all doing at every minute*. Sokal would do well to read the current issue of *New Scientist* (May 8th, 2010) which recounts in detail the 'weirdness' of the quantum world. We are in the middle of a real (which includes 'inward' as well as 'outward things'), which we may question as long as we like but which we will never match our 'singular' words that overlap but never coincide upon the mutually imagined 'referents'. So the prejudice takes its source not only from the desire to avoid the supposed suspicion of the other, but the more deep-seated fear that one's *self* is open to doubt, that one's identity is forever in question. Instead of welcoming that uncertainty as a guarantee of being human, being engaged in the sublime and thrilling game of language, the fundamentalist projects his or her fear outside and lodges it in a hatred of a scapegoat.

A personal note to show the effect of the suspicion: I have a philosophical ally with whom I share many beliefs about

---

[3]   William Wordsworth, 'Ode on Intimations of Immortality' lines 141–7.

perception—yet he has never expressed any agreement with this particular claim. But it is not that that is worth the comment, but rather the fact that, over the years, *he has produced no argument whatsoever to refute it.* And I can add, neither has anyone else in the philosophical community. It could, of course, be that it is not worth the refuting because the objections are so obvious. I am left in my ignorance to wonder what they might be, and to fall back on the explanation of this suspect suspicion that I have just given. Someone must put me out of my ignorance at last, mustn't they? I say 'at last', because I first introduced the Bomb-Disposers Argument into the philosophical conversation in 1990 (Wright, 1990, 73–8).

At least one can try to anticipate yet another unspoken objection. Does not rejection of the objectivity of singular entities fly in the face of the fact that human knowledge has undeniably progressed, that our 'reality' picture obviously bears what seems a close relation to the real; otherwise, we would be attended with endless disasters owing to misperception, to verbal misconstruction? Why yes, one must admit that the percepts that our ancestors have passed on to us have daily their success: Ernst von Glasersfeld uses the word 'viable' for our daily habitual applications of words to the real (Glasersfeld, 1984, 25). Language is endlessly adapting itself in history, evolving through our mutual corrections to keep pace with change. What this attests to, however, is that the flows in the real, rapid, slow or viscous in relation to our human purposes, change at a rate which is often hardly perceptible when tested against our current fears and desires. Ask what the word 'ship' meant in 600 A.D. and what it means now. It is easy to forget how inconstant and parochial those fears and desires are, and how much there is that we do not attend to because it is of no immediate interest to us. Add to this the fact that, even where agreement is attested to by all, there are bound to be sensory and perceptual differences which did not happen to become salient on some given occasion. It is more than we are ignoring them — we do not know that they are there to be ignored. Furthermore, this objection forgets that what is being rejected in the present theory is the *pure singularity* of the 'entities' we home in on. That impossible singularity, the mutual *imagining* of which is necessary for speech, is evidence of the equally imagined perfect goal of all our thought, all our fears and desires.

Terry Eagleton has recently pointed out this oddity about our intentions (Eagleton, 2010, 104–5), that, if one tries to state what one has done a particular action for, say what one's underlying purpose was, the result is an endless list, since every minor purpose can be shown to be contributing to some further one. The philosopher J.L. Austin noted this fuzziness about intentions for human beings:

> Should we say, are we saying, that he took her money, or that he robbed her? That he knocked a ball into a hole, or that he sank a putt? That he said, 'Done', or that he accepted an offer? How far, that is, are motives, intentions and conventions to be part of the descriptions of actions? (Austin, 1970, 201).

But it is not just a matter of alternative descriptions: intentions are capable of ever wider definition. For example, you decide to stop working and have a cup of tea. The action is not only describable by saying that you were thirsty, for your choice of tea is a reflection of your being fond of that drink, and perhaps of your being English or Indian. But one could add that without the drink you would not be in so good a state for going on with your work, nor can one deny that it contributes to your state of health and state of mind, and that without that health you would not be able to continue with all your deeper intentions, perhaps today the writing of a novel which is to highlight the unsatisfactory conditions of people condemned to the underclass, and also to bring them to political notice just before an election, which brings in your intentions vis-à-vis the society you are a member of, etc., etc. Another philosopher, Joel Feinberg, has dubbed this extending of intention into the future the 'Accordion Effect':

> This well-known feature of our language, whereby a man's actions can be described as narrowly or as broadly as we please, I propose to call the 'accordion effect', because an act, like the folding musical instrument, can be squeezed down to a minimum or else stretched out (Feinberg, 1964, 146).

(He gives part of the answer to the questions surrounding this odd feature of language in that almost unnoticed little interjection 'as we please'.) The accordion is stretched out by our providing wider and wider explanations of the intentional context. But there is a question that Feinberg did not ask: Is there the assumption that there is some *one* fixed fully open position, which, although a few of the bellow pleats are tattered, still represents a 'totality' of understanding which touches the world securely at its fully extended edges? In view of this, the perfect singularity of any entity can be seen to be only a mirage of this final agreement, which itself is a mirage, since there can be no merging of all our desires that would find focus on some 'one' thing, self or person.

Another part of the answer as to why the 'as if' is taken for real is that one can feel so much safer if the incalculable shiftings of the hazardous real are just due to our uncertain

identifications, and that a secure haven, as well as a guid-
ing, 'omniscient', divine Father, will, if we hold on long
enough, show himself at last and reveal all the divine singu-
larities of the world to our 'knowledge'. I am arguing that
'divine' here means *imagined in mutual faith*. It is only a
proper faith that can bestow that 'sacred' quality. It is very
frightening indeed to entertain the thought that the real
might *not* be the ordered system governed by 'laws' that we
hope it is, instead of the system only being an instrument of
our hope. So the 'faith' of the old-religious is a completely
unsubstantiated taking-to-be-real of the 'as if', of what is
only a mutual *taking-for-granted*. In particular for them, it
has the added advantage of shoring up their present notion
of their own identity. They want the trust required by the
performance of a statement to be secure *for both self and the
other*, and that is plainly not faith.

Indeed, one objection that has been put to the theory[4] was
to dismiss the 'perspectival' differences between person
and person because they were 'trivial' and could fairly be
neglected; he said that they were 'taken for granted' and
could be laid aside as of no concern. I have elsewhere, and
more than once, drawn attention to that phrasal verb 'take
for' in that phrase 'take for granted' (Wright, 2005, 111–13).
It is used in situations that are ambiguous — 'It was so foggy
I *took* him *for* his brother'. So — we haven't in fact 'granted' at
all — we are together only hoping that we have aligned our
differing aims and intentions. Consider what 'to grant'
means: that you are *assuming* that nothing the other does
will seriously disturb your hopes and plans. But every statement we make in the hope of informing someone begins

[4]   By Andrew Bartlett in a response at a Generative Anthropology
conference, Salt Lake City, 2010.

with this strictly false assumption of our both homing in on *the very same thing*. If we didn't do that, our attempts at reference would never overlap; our would-be-co-operative actions could never work in harness together.

Another way of helping someone who doubts this analysis to see what is being claimed is to draw attention to the following feature of the co-operative process that is 'knowledge'. The word 'granted' is the phrase 'take for granted' has a distinct implication that cannot be ignored. If you yourself have been tempted to dismiss this theory with that phrase, with its comforting sense of habitual and customary 'objective' security, consider that one cannot shut one's eyes to the fact that, if one *grants* something, the situation involves *more than one person*. You are granting *to another person* that any differences between your perception and theirs is timelessly of no account. You have both in hopeful imagination *counted* up to one; you both are behaving *as if* there is one entity, one referent before you both, the same for both of you. But the convergence can never be achieved precisely because it is a timeless, ideal, logical singularity that cannot exist, that cannot include all the sensory and perceptual criteria particular to each of you. The Bomb-Disposers cannot escape the peculiarities of their own machines, however much they behave as if those differences did not exist. That is why, just now, I put 'knowledge' in inverted commas. Knowledge is *always* fraught with ambiguity because it is a temporary compromise *across persons*, and can never, as a co-operative process, arrive at a perfect superimposition of understanding. It is irredeemably dual. For it rides on language and language exists to update others (hopefully), and one cannot update unless one has a *different* understanding of something than someone else; recall Dilthey's remark that, if we agreed on everything, there would be no reason to speak. The move to 'taking for granted' demands trust, and it is incumbent upon us to bear in mind that the risks that the real may make actual require us ethically to turn that 'trust' into faith.

Ironic situations in plays and novels often occur when the partners in dialogue do not know that they are referring to entirely different bits of the world which results in a mix-up of their motivations, a dire case of what we call 'cross-purposes'. A good example is the confusion in Shakespeare's *Twelfth Night* when, in the pre-arranged duel, Sir Toby and Sir Andrew *take* Sebastian *for* Cesario-Viola — their misconstruction ends with Sir Andrew coming on stage crying for a surgeon for Sir Toby, for 'he' they *took for* a 'coward' turned out to be 'the devil incardinate' (sic). The 'granting' definitely didn't work out there, nor can it ever in full. Our purposes always 'cross'. Andrew Bartlett, nevertheless, did show in the vigorous way in which he expressed himself, a deep commitment to the trust that language and, hence, life, requires: it is just that faith requires an acknowledgement of the risks, in the self, other selves, and the world, which can be quite innocently unexpected. The real at its most unthreatening may conceal the greatest dangers; we have only apparently tamed it.

The greatest irony here is, of course, that the perfect singularity of every entity, and, hence, the 'truth' of every 'word', has, nevertheless, to be the focus of our real, impossible faith. The mathematical order is the framework of the mutual fiction. Mathematics and pure logic are thus the most fictive of human activities. The drama of human life cannot proceed unless we maintain the imagined, 'divine' interlocking of our understandings. The logical 'must', being a fictive creation of that mutual faith, is hiding itself like the supposed agreement at the start of a joke, which is why it appears so divorced from human wish and aversion, the very reason it is called 'pure'. Shakespeare continually reminds us that the Fool with his jokes is 'not altogether fool' (*King Lear*, I, iv, 154).

Having followed the argument to this point, whether or not you have accepted it, you may have noticed how, in placing our life, our selves, our society and our knowledge as pre-eminently matters of dialogue between two or more of us, the conclusion leads to a radical rejection of individualism, of the notion of a single, objective, fully self-conscious mind active in the body. Singularity is a necessary catalyst in language, one which has to be mutually imagined for language to allow the partial convergence of our differing understandings of the real, whether inside or outside of our bodies, but which has no reality except that of that imagining itself in the material brains that perform it. So the argument can present itself as a last move in *Copernican* thought—first, Copernicus, banishing man from the centre of the universe; second, Immanuel Kant seeing all knowledge of self, other persons and things as created by an individual mind from the 'manifold' of the senses, not as objectively given; third, the present argument, dislodging the erstwhile singular ego from the throne it has too long occupied. *And, dear reader, that includes 'yours'.*

Five

Identity, Truth and Love

You can see why the would-be religious are up in arms as soon as you argue that words are not the secure things we have mutually *to imagine* them; Pope Benedict calls you a 'relativist'; others will add 'solipsist'. John McDowell, the philosopher, claims that you have lost your hold on the real if you argue that all our identifications are only viable selections from the chaos of your sensory fields. The commitment to singularity is very clear in McDowell's thought, evidencing itself in his repeated claim that everything is 'thus-and-so', that is, existing in logical clarity independently of our choices (McDowell, 1994, 42).[1] Without knowing it, deep down the old-religious take it, as I have just said, to be an attack on our trust in each other, on social cohesion itself—but this is to try to ignore the terrible dangers for which a proper faith is prepared, the only kind of faith that can keep 'social cohesion' as the (unattainable) ideal. It is amusing that they also ignore the significance that I noted above (pp. 14–15) of the *pleasant* surprises that the real sometimes is benevolent enough to bestow. In this case, the

---

[1]   Note the similarity to Brandom's view, his colleague at the University of Pittsburgh.

temptation for them, of course, is to believe that the good result was implied all the time by their interpretation of events and so can be counted as a confirmation of 'objective singularity' — another hidden oxymoron.

The most intimate danger is *the discovery of some part of the real inside one's 'self'* for it throws one's identity into the crucible. In the *Avatar* film, Jake Sully — 'I am not sure who I am any more' — was prepared for radical uncertainty about his 'self'. As I said earlier, the fear surfaces in the conscious mind in the search for a scapegoat on which to lodge itself. Witness some 'holy men' who make a fuss about women as bishops, homosexuals as ayatollahs; it is distinctly similar to the denial of nationality to gypsies or Jews or Palestinians. The 'holy men' have to give themselves a false ego-integrity by distinguishing themselves from *what they are not*. There has even in England this year a ludicrous attempt (in a Tesco advertisement) to bully ginger-headed people! Perhaps if Hitler had succeeded in killing off all the Jews and the gypsies and the homosexuals and the black people and the disabled and the mentally deficient and the insane, he could have started on the *Rotschöpfe*, the 'copperknobs' — for, as everyone knows, 'Aryans' have fair hair. As I once pointed out to a group of children who were bullying a child with his arm in plaster cast, Hitler would have gone on looking for scapegoats different from himself *until he was the last person left alive.*

What is worse in the old-religious view of things is that their kind of 'faith' hides the actual nature of what a proper faith should be, which is to be prepared for everything one has 'taken for' granted to turn out to be a radical disappointment. This implies being prepared for the moment at which, if you love someone, you may find that some kind of sacrifice is the only path worthy the choosing – a choice which, with you as martyr, will *not* be divinely rewarded by an eternal joy, but only the hope that one's example may possibly emerge as an example for others later in the history of the drama of the great human imagining. It may not glorify you, for you may be nameless, like those who freely took the place of others in the ovens of Auschwitz. Their example still inspires, anonymity or no. *One doesn't do good in order to be personally rewarded, even in posthumous reputation.*

So it is no use thinking that a blind trust in either the other's 'word' or your own can guarantee safety. Sincerity is not enough. Tony Blair can't use 'sincerity' as a 'Get-out-of-jail-free' card, for the game is more subtle than Monopoly; the meaning of words cannot be monopolized. What being a speaker demands is faith in every word, not 'sincerity'. Nor can one claim to have discovered a final 'truth', for that hoped-for coincidence of all our separate perspectives can never be reached, though we must all behave as if it can, as a sign of our love. To behave *as if* there is a heaven is one thing; it is thus a proof of faith – to believe that there *is* one is to be already in a fool's paradise, hobbled by fear. Tony Blair, by the way, wants to unify all 'faiths': the present proposal is the only way of doing it.

The word 'truth' actually comes from the word 'troth' (*sworn trust*), and we often use 'truth' for faith: 'Oh, love, let us be true to one another', as Matthew Arnold put it, fearful that faith was 'retreating down the vast edges drear and naked shingles of the world'. He – and Tennyson in *In Memoriam* – should not have been so pessimistic, for, although old religions may be moribund, every time you speak, the chance of real faith is offered. As I have already said elsewhere, *troth comes before truth, and love before troth*

(Wright, 2005, 228). It is noteworthy that in what is perhaps the most recent professional philosophical book on truth, at all points the singularity of what is referred to is never the focus of the arguments, but is accepted as a *sine qua non*, fact attested to by the universal use of symbolic logic throughout and continual reference to those entities the objective 'truth-makers' that exist to be referred to (Lowe and Rami, 2009). It is we who are the 'truth-makers'.

Philip Larkin ended his 'An Arundel Tomb' poem with the line 'What survives of us is love'. One can certainly say that one's contribution to the ongoing human drama persists in the influences, both slight and considerable, your life has had upon other people. 'You' will still be active in the living drama, and 'spiritual' in your imagined character. If you have shown love, this is what the best of 'God' and 'Heaven' can be, but, unfortunately, since the great game can be badly played, also the worst of 'the Devil' and 'Hell', where 'what survives of you' is hate. The 'spirit' of Hitler is still active in some people today. In primitive versions of Christianity, devils were as immortal as any other being.

When Shakespeare in his sonnets repeatedly invokes his poems as immortalizing his love, there was a sense in which he was being, not hyperbolically fanciful, but literal: 'In black ink my love may still shine bright' makes his love enter the living play now as we read his words. But, as stories in the Gothic genre make plain, the great Story as enacted now can be corrupted. Another poet, the mad John Clare, when in later life he became insane, believed himself overcome by 'blue devils'. The notion of 'diabolical possession' is accepted as a real possibility — acted on this very week in the eastern Congo, where 'witch-children' are being killed, having been first tortured into confessing that they are 'avatars' possessed by demons.

Games, as children know, have to be played with the utmost seriousness, that is, *without ever falling into superstitious conviction* — for example, they won't think much of the child playing a Na'vi warrior who really cries when he is taken prisoner. Faith cannot be achieved by someone who can't face up to there being no reward for his or her supposedly 'single' soul. You are not in the least single, for something of 'your' own part in the play escapes 'you' at this very moment. Other people have a say in who you are. 'Your' identity is in play.[2] The only soul you have is the one you and those around you create in the human game, certainly as invisible, as 'spiritual' a soul as Plato would wish, and it is really going on in the game, as really as any play on in the National Theatre. This makes England a National Theatre — the World an International Theatre. This is what the 'spiritual' always has been anyway. We can quote Neytiri, Jake Sully's Na'vi lover: 'Spirit is all that matters'. One has to repeat, though, that, in spite of having its being in all our imaginations, the great drama has serious outcomes in the real and can be played with good *or bad* results so we must beware of divinizing 'spirit' instead of playing it. Incidentally, the word 'matter' as a verb meaning *to be important, to be foremost in one's interests* derives metaphorically from 'matter' as meaning *the basic constituent of the universe*, possibly itself metaphorically from words meaning *wood* or *mother*, wood suggestive of that which something is made, mother standing as the formative origin. So here Neytiri's

---

[2]   This, by the way, is why solipsism, thinking that the only real thing is you, a *solus-ipse*, 'solitary self', *is actually impossible*, a new conclusion which does away with one accusation commonly levelled at this theory.

use of 'matters' implies a hoped-for final aim that tran-
scends 'one's' immediate goals.

   In case anyone thinks that in describing life as a play one
forfeits all relevance to the real, recall that, in watching a
play, although one is aware that the whole is a performance
of an 'as if' world, the play as a play does have relevance for
our lived experience. We are all engaged in the hopeful
construction of a system that should induce better selves,
and, thus, better communities, and the play should extend
that future imagined world in the bodies that are to be part
of the real.

Six

What is so Special about Avatarhood then?

Since your sense of being a 'single' person 'you' owe to the language-game and not to 'your' body, 'you', as avatar, the hypothetical construct, cannot *own* 'your' body, even though all the fears and desires, pains and pleasures, sights and sounds are produced by it. You actually know vanishingly little about it. A would-be 'single' person — call it a soul, if you like — has been set up in it by all those who have talked and gestured to you, but the body still remains stubbornly part of the real, in that no different from what it will be in the grave, and was before 'you' WAS set up in it by others — which, by the way, certainly did *not* occur at the moment of conception, despite the conviction of 'pro-lifers'. The only conclusion is that, 'you' *actually IS an avatar*, an imagined region of the great game, that others have hope-fully established in that body, trusting 'it' will really play, using that body as a touchstone of the rules, to the best of 'its' ability — that is, with faith. 'It' was put in inverted com-mas just now because there can obviously be no one version of it common to all parents, relatives, teachers, friends, etc.

who have a part in inculcating it across different children. There is certainly no 'real body' *somewhere else* operating your body (as in *Avatar*, *The Matrix*, and *Surrogates*) — the source of the ideals that have established the 'YOU' is the ongoing game-drama and all its historical roots and future plans, which, fortunately, though only in principle, is always open to allowing the body to re-direct them or, at least, ignore them. The ideal 'YOUs' are themselves fictive, yet are really at work. Like all other 'entities', of course, their 'singularity' is an illusion, albeit pragmatically necessary as 'an imagined region of the great game'. Nevertheless, the hope of those who inculcated the 'self' in this body which you call yours was that its differences would make their special contribution to the human play.

It has been pointed out to me by the sociologist Marcin Smietana (personal communication) that there is a parallel here with George Herbert Mead's distinction between the 'I' and the 'Me' (Mead, 1934, 174–8, 197). All the roles and the rules of the self-specification become embraced for the individual agent in a 'symbolized unity' that Mead calls 'the generalized other' (ibid., 154), and in the symbolic interaction of the body with the requirements of this generalized other the body has to decide which of them it is to adopt, reject or adjust. It is clear that this generalized other is the sedimenting, we might say, of what has been conveyed to you by all those with whom you have 'talked and gestured'. Mead calls the 'Me' the past, already established requirements that are responsible for the whole notion of a self, and would define it completely, and the 'I' the 'novel reply' of the body to them, to what the generalized other would have it be (ibid., 197). He calls it a creative response and not a conditioned one because the body always has the freedom in the double-avatar situation to take up a different and perhaps new attitude to the external requirement; as he puts it, there seem to be 'alternative courses of action' (ibid., 177). It cannot escape the notion of Self without pathological results, but it can escape the particularity of the criteria the system attempts to impose because there is no way, in the double-avatar situation, of making them precise. Incidentally, Mead did not say, but could have done, that 'the generalized other' has been called 'God'.

In its software (a useful metaphor our predecessors did not have), 'It' contains suggested specifications about ethical behaviour, relations to kin and other people, gender, social role, local and national identity, cultural preferences, language skills, and more, all linked in the notion of a self, a *single* origin of desires and aversions so guided. But none of these deliver singularity-as-real. Even within language itself, with the ideal of 'a' speaker and hearers, a statement, however corrective of the public understanding, remains a statement that attempts to harmonize what can never reach a perfect concord, *a fortiori* about the speaker him- or herself.

'It' is not like the controller of a 'drone' (an unmanned military aircraft) because he, sitting in the US, doesn't feel any pains or pleasures in Afghanistan — he is a *mock*-avatar: the body, on the other hand, provides 'you', as it did Jake Sully, with a means of testing out what is being constructed in the body, and the right to propose adjustments of the language, thus of the authority of social system itself, which is, anyway, forever in flux. It is never the unquestionable lodgement of 'the Good': sometimes it may produce good results, sometimes not — and sometimes, tragically, it may not be possible to apportion 'the Good' safely to the aims of either the system or the body. 'God' is never 'on one's side'.

In either case, 'self' or 'generalized other', there is no 'one' to be on the side of! Mead saw the interplay of conflict and consensus, both within the self and between self and society as all part of 'the process of human social evolution' (ibid., 309).

The feeling body's key place in the scheme is inversely highlighted by the fact that Jake Sully is a cripple; he escapes the limitations of his disability in inhabiting his Na'vi avatar. Our attention is drawn to this when he celebrates his temporary release on his first entering his Na'vi body by ignoring the warnings of the biological researchers in the lab and runs out into the open air, running and jumping in delight. The body's importance is also emphasized when Colonel Quaritch, in order to ensure Jake's loyalty, offers him an expensive future medical operation to restore his control over his real legs. The longer the 'You' software is in the body, already marked by the character one's mentors have set up in it, the more it takes on the peculiar character of that body and its history. After all, the body is where the results show up, as was just remarked upon, where suffering and joy go on, where the sacrifices are felt; it provides the test-bed. Jake Sully fell in love. So did Sam Tyler in his '1973'. This is part of what our incarnation means.

Colonel Quaritch, sitting in his *Matrix*-style robot machine, his 'Amplified Mobility Platform Suit', like the driver of Evans's mechanical digger, was only a mock-avatar: he didn't feel what his metal arms came in contact with. Neither do the totalitarian dictators as they make their own educational specifications of what 'selves' should be; they are utterly indifferent to how a subject feels as that subject is manipulated with their mechanical arms. In the story of the film the Na'vi were real avatars to the animals when they connected their neural nets directly, in the bonding known as 'tsahaylu', to those of the 'direhorses', or the great flying reptiles, the Ikran, or the great Leonopteryx when the rider becomes the mythical saviour Toruk Macto (*'Rider of the Last Shadow'*), — you know that the Na'vi, unlike US drone operatives, could *feel the flying* — as well as any hurt. Sam Tyler, in *Life on Mars*, discovered what to do with his life when he realized that it was in 1973 and not in 2006 that he felt hurt when his finger was injured. Similarly, in *Surrogates*, for the Bruce Willis figure, Tom Greer, the power to feel pain and pleasure becomes the touchstone for distinguishing the avatars from human beings.

Without the software, of course, there is no 'self', good or bad. Those unfortunate 'feral' children ('The Wild Boy of Aveyron', Caspar Hauser) who were brought up away from all human contact via language, were not human at all. They were like an Ikran without an avatar-rider. The real reason 'pro-lifers' cannot understand this is because they want the software to be in the body from the start, body and 'soul' magically identical, ready to be guided by a perfect 'Good', also magically the same for body and society, so that the pure 'authority' will be able to order what the pure 'freedom' desires — which can be said to constitute *totalitarian religion*. Easy now to comprehend why the old-religious believe that we 'are made in God's image', for our own singularity has to be imagined in the same way as does every other entity, and is as dependent upon faith as any-'thing' else.

But avatarhood, incarnation, is an experiment the outcome of which may alter sometimes the 'authority', sometimes the 'free desire', sometimes both. There is no guarantee that Mead's 'generalized other', the would-be god that has implanted all the self-specifications according to the given wisdom of the time, should have got it right for all bodies. Incidentally, if in a bodily system a pure authority did order what a pure freedom desired, so that there could never be any changing of mind, the result would be a Cameronian 'terminator' — Arnie was showing you what the final aim of a pro-lifer's philosophy actually is! But for us, as experimenting avatars, 'free will', so much the centre of endless theological debate, is here given an understandable lodging in this theory, for there is no final 'authority' which could interfere with our choices (or know them 'omnisciently' beforehand!) — we are, whether we like it or not, continuously involved in trying to define it for ever! Does this solve the centuries-long 'Free Will-Predestination' chestnut, or doesn't it? Of course, by the same token, the age-old paradoxes, from Zeno onwards, have also been given the final comeuppance, the reason being that they all depend on trying to place agreed finite boundaries on the boundless, especially where there is no possibility, because of the infinitesimal smallness of the supposed 'referent', to reach a *mutual* agreement at all.[1]

So all 'persons' have their basis in imagination since we all work on a 'self'-hypothesis. We are not so much *social*-constructionists, as *soul*-constructionists. It is not entirely a coincidence that the very word 'person' should come from a Greek word meaning *mask*, alluding to the masks worn by Greek actors. Further back in time, the word originates from the meaning *through-sound*, the sound of the human voice, the instrument of language, what makes us human, coming 'through' the actor's mask, that is, through the animal mask of the face, *from the incarnated 'you'-avatar.*

---

[1]   See, for the untying of those knots, Wright, 2005, 171–88.

Seven

What must we do now?

So faith has to be performed as a myth in real time, as a drama in progress, a 'language-game' that may have no winners. Yet we must all play our avatar-parts in that drama as if it were literal, our faith as a promise of our being ready for unexpected sacrifice for those we love, which means that we know that it is not literal.

Obsession with a rigid self is *an avoidance of faith* that is basically craven for all its macho bombast about courage — for then we become the 'dream-demons' the Na'vi tribe feared. Of course, in England, 'faith schools', if you now accept this new definition of 'faith', must now be called 'superstition schools', for the real risk, out of fear, is being concealed from those taught in them. It is indeed cowardly to hold to fundamentalist conviction about a fixed identity for things or persons or selves, to cultist or racist or misogynist or homophobic or xenophobic or, as Auschwitz demonstrated, dysmorphophobic ('deformity/disabled-phobic') conviction — of which two disturbing examples leading to deaths have recently been in the news on our British TV screens — or gerontophobic — evidenced in the recent arsonist attacks in the English Midlands on mobility vehicles for the aged. It is worth pointing out that it is the *very same* motivation that lies behind the bullying at South Hadley High School in Massachusetts this month (March, 2010) that led to the suicide of a female Irish student (jeers of 'Irish slut', 'Irish whore', characterized the bullying, revealing the connection between bodily desire and its would-be-moral guidance; ironically, South Hadley was George Herbert Mead's birthplace). We need to stress the link across all of these types of identity-fear, and make the perpetrators see it.

Here the theory could be said to dovetail, though not completely, with Terry Eagleton's account of evil, though whether he would accept this philosophical support is another matter (Eagleton, 2010). He sees evil as neither conditioned by social influences, the self as 'machine', nor as motivated by an anarchic ego, the self as 'monster'. Under the present explanation, the social influence, though responsible for implanting the whole apparatus of self and social relation, and without which there could be no human self, cannot beforehand embrace all that the body can contribute to the workings of that very social system, and, in particular to the language that is the core of the (would-be) reciprocal process.

Therein lies our responsibility, for we cannot detach our own selfhood from our speech with others, since we are engaged in the endless defining of that selfhood (and of that of others). I argue that it is *the cowardly aversion from a true faith* that leads to the evil excesses of the 'machines' of distorted control, as in Hitler, or of the 'monsters' of uncontrolled sadism, as in the recent case of torture by the two boys in Edlington in Yorkshire. Note that in neither case does moral responsibility fail to be an option available to bodies at either pole of this spectrum. What is significant is that for both — and these particular examples prove it — the basic need for myth and fantasy becomes wholly perverted from its right use. It is worth noting that Eagleton himself uses the avatar metaphor in its 'mock-avatar' form (like Colonel Quaritch in his 'Mobility Platform') for an evil person being out of harmony with his body, a body which 'is no part of his identity' (Eagleton, 2010, 21).

There is intense irony in Pope Benedict[1] berating what he calls a 'dictatorship of relativism that does not recognize anything as definitive and whose ultimate goal consists only of one's own ego and desires', when it is the superstition of absolute certainty that informs the fear-stricken dictators among us, and the courageous acceptance of uncertainty that characterizes a true faith that can countenance the sacrifice of what one has taken to be 'one's desires'.

As an aid in a proper performance of the game, how refreshing to see on 'Pandora' what holding to myth, with its poetry and music and dance, can do for one's determination to face sacrifice. When everything turns out right in James Cameron's fairy-tale ending, with the last shot of the film plainly a defeat of death (Jake Sully restored alive and permanently to his Na'vi body), we can interpret it as a childlike presentation of our impossible hope, our 'unobtanium', 'something evermore about to be' (William Wordsworth, *The Prelude* [1850], VI, 608). It is definitely not to be seen as symbolizing a *superstitious* immortality, for that hides the *real* one that is actually going on now in the great play, at the very same time as the body remains the dust from whence it came. Paradoxical as though it sounds, it is fair to say that, in one sense, the body is 'dead' already,

[1]   In a sermon in St. Peter's Basilica, 18th April, 2005.

the sense in which it has always been a part of the wordless real, before birth, during 'life', and after.

As was concluded above, 'your' essence is part of the game now and will remain so after the dispersal of the real in 'your' body. The single 'entities' imagined in the game are not real, *but the imagining of them itself is.* 'King Lear' is not a real person, but *the imagining of him together*, by both actors and audience at Stratford tonight, is. Similarly, one can reject the idea of a 'spiritual soul' and say that it is an entirely imagined notion, but one has to acknowledge the real-as-present in the imagining of that imaginary entity. Its 'spiritual' nature, invisible, and out of scientific reach as has been conceived of up to now, is easily understood as the consequence of its *fictive* nature, but its creation-as-fictive does remain within the scope of a more enlightened scientific inquiry, one open to *examining what constitutes play,* and that play has real effects.

'One' need not fear, like Thomas Hardy in his poem 'He prefers her earthly', that after death his wife's spirit is floating around in the sunset sky. 'Her soul' was always really-imagined, and will remain so in the strata of posterity's active memories as the game continues to be played.

> Our echoes roll from soul to soul
> And grow for ever and for ever.[2]

So, *pace* Onfray's warnings about it being 'a really deadly sin' to believe in an after-life, there is a way of giving it a sensible interpretation that has no taint of superstitious belief in it. All memories, by this light, are, as all recognitions are, mutual guesses too, and so should be embraced by the challenge of faith. The fundamentalists can't get their heads round the notion that God, the guarantor of all identities (as

---

[2]   Tennyson, 'The splendour falls from castle walls', ll.15–16.

Bishop Berkeley believed) is a *useful* and *actual* mutual FIC-
TION. The performing of the fiction is real. No wonder the
Taliban destroyed the Buddha statue—one mustn't make
images of God—it is too close to the truth. The 'dream' of life
is what we are all contributing to in our good and bad ways,
but it is not an 'insubstantial' dream, but one in which we
are all 'actors' (Shakespeare, *The Tempest*, IV, I, 147–57).

By this time, you should have realized that every identification you make with the help of language, from the page in
front of you now to yourself as person, should be hopefully
sustained out of the incalculable real by faith—and not by a
complacent conviction about its 'objectivity' being identical
with 'its' existence. There are no 'its' in existence. It is no
surprise that, out of that false assurance, the religions have
said that God the Creator is everywhere. Our ancestors
have handed on to us a vast range of 'objectifications', the
majority of which so far have worked with the real, but we
must not forget that we have only achieve a tentative viability with all of them, because they are constituted by *sharing*
what can never coalesce. Both 'objecti*fication*' and even the
word '*fact*' come from the Latin verb *facere*, 'to make'. So
every-'thing' you recognize, including your-'self', is a
co-operatively made, human selection. This bears out the
late Richard Gregory's assertion, that every percept was of
the nature of a hypothesis (Gregory, 1993). The only correction here is, of course, as was pointed out earlier, is that '*the*
hypothesis' is not strictly single, made by one isolated ego,
but a hidden convergence of as many 'hypotheses' as are
persons engaged in the 'identification', the co-operative
apportioning of 'identity' to a region of the real.

Earlier (pp. 17–20) it was argued that to take 'the referent'
as an actually existing singular entity, the same for all

observers, was quite otiose since our purposes are served just as much by behaving *as if* there were a singular referent. There was also the unavoidable implication that to believe in the singular referent was unethical because it brought with it a blindness to the risks and responsibilities of faith. One can add here that this timid fixation on a given objectivity for any entity is now recognizable as *superstition*. Rather than face up with courage to what faith requires of us the objectivist relies on what is frankly a soothing, not to say dulling, illusion, the effect of which is to conceal the taxing obligations that can emerge in the exchanges of language. I fail to see the difference here between the objectivists, the 'direct realists' as they call themselves, and devotees of astrology, numerology or the reading of tarot cards. If any objectivists are now wincing at what may seem a bizarre description of their position, it behoves them to address the criticism and not ignore it.

It is also easy to see now why the creationists think that 'God' has created every-'thing', for the faith of language performed by our ancestors has indeed chosen all those parts of the real that we familiarly 'recognize' together. Why do you think that ancestors were so important for many 'primitive' tribes? What 'He' didn't do, of course, is *create the real*, the 'chaos', *from which* those 'entities' were and are *at this moment* being mutually chosen, and which *ought to be* an earnest of the faith of both our ancestors and ourselves. It is equally easy to see why in the past the Idealists in philosophy believed that all reality could be encompassed by the word, that it was all 'spiritual' and not material. They completely ignore the necessity for mutual faith, unconsciously afraid of the risks it brings with it as it has to deal with what always remains outside our knowledge. I heard 'the Daily Prayer' this morning on the BBC: the Anglican vicar appealed to 'the great design in the heavens' as a sign of 'God's greatness': what it actually shows is the astonishing, ages-long struggle of man- and woman-kind to fix words on the wordless, and, since a huge, though partial, success has been achieved, we are right to lodge some of our hope upon that achievement, the partial convergence of those hypotheses that have gained some measure of success, while knowing it remains only a viable construct, ever open to amendment.

Thus, as we saw in our discussion of Harman's, McDowell's and Brandom's commitment to given 'objectivity', *objectivity and existence come apart* (Wright, 2005, 119). What this implies is that there is plenty of what you are sensing at the moment that has *not* been named by 'God' (or positivistic scientists, still haunted by the Enlightenment), and even inside what has, indeed, what seems most unthreatening, danger may hide — and, as was pointed out before, unexpected pleasant surprises! No wonder children, from Freud's 'Fort-Da!' onwards, enjoy practical jokes that promise disaster only to replace it with delight. Chaos is close. It didn't disappear, as 'Genesis' has it, at 'the Creation of the World' because we are all creating our shared world out of the chaos *now*. All recognizable entities are constructed co-operatively, a social act. The chaos, however, that from which we are creating these entities, both objects and selves, remains in part outside our knowing. The automatic registering that our senses do of the mindless input, strikes our sense organs all the time whether we

attend to it or not. Both the sensation and what it is caused
by externally are equally mindless.[3]

> The eye — it cannot choose but see;
> We cannot bid the ear be still;
> Our bodies feel, where'er they be,
> Against or with our will.[4]

In the case of some persons suffering brain-damage, the
so-called condition of 'agnosia' (i.e. *no-knowing*), they are
quite unable to perceive or name anything in the sensory
input. In some possible mutant birth in an advanced animal,
a birth in which the neural connections between sensation,
motivation and memory did not exist, sensing, the 'qualia',
even of a most vivid character, could be going on without
any consciousness being involved. Nothing surprising in
this, for even now I may open a drawer looking for a green
cuff-link and be completely unaware that a red tie lies
beside it, that is, red would be part of my visual field but not
part of my consciousness (see Wright, 1996, 30–1).

Philosophers have called this the 'non-epistemic' input,
that is, a *'no-knowledge'* input, just a mass of *evidence* that we
may or may not interpret. It is just like the evidence that a
detective works on: a depression in the ground is a sign to
Ian Rankin's detective John Rebus that a woman wearing
shoes bought at Russell and Bromley's in Edinburgh has
just passed by, but none of this is noticed by his assistant
constable. Evidence is not information: none of it comes
conveniently labelled with words; Mead called it 'the bare
thereness of the world', its state before people in their social
group have sorted out their 'objects' and 'selves' (Mead,
1934, 135–6). Jorge Luis Borges in his story 'Funes the

---

[3]   For the philosopher-reader, we can add that this implies that qualia,
      the internal sensory registrations, are not in themselves *conscious*.

[4]   William Wordsworth, 'Expostulation and Reply' v.

Memorious' presents a case of someone so overwhelmed by the rich detail of the sensory chaos as to be unable to handle the world successfully, a literary allegory of our own partial success. In spite of the Idealist bid for certainty in naming, mind cannot capture all of matter.

The whole 'objective world', what we unthinkingly call *'reality'*, is actually part of the game, while the board it is played on, *the real*, isn't. Is it not our constant hope is that someone else will notice some vital detail in the real that we have not?[5] By the way, notice that these reflections dispose of the old Berkleyan puzzle about whether the 'tree in the quad' is still there when no one is looking at it. The real out of which anyone's 'tree' can be selected (should they be in the quad) is certainly present, but what we call 'the tree' can only be caught up in our fields of attention if people are present looking in the direction of that fuzzy region. With no one there, chaos, the mindless, reigns.

It is just like a set of scientists coming up with theories that 'identify objects': these work in part but don't capture fully what is going on. Take the example of Victorian astronomers, before Einstein, operating with Newton's Laws. We are all like those Victorian astronomers, confidently making predictions about the self- and person-'planets' — and all the 'object-stars' as well — and, though our whole Newtonian theory is wide of the mark, *yet every day we see those predictions apparently 'confirmed'*. In Ptolemy's time no one doubted the 'objectivity' of those 'epicycles' that the outer planets went twirling through. As I said before, the real, however lumpy and fragmentary and viscous, does seem to tolerate many of our words, at least for

---

[5]   For more about the evidence, the 'chaos', the non-epistemic, see Wright, 2008, 8–22, 345–50.

the time being. However, two articles in the current *New Scientist* (May 6th, 2010) both throw doubt upon the notion that words will finally capture the 'truth' about the universe. Marcelo Gleiser rejects the idea of aiming at a 'theory of everything' (Gleiser, 2010, 28); the only possible 'theory of every-'thing', I would say, is the theory you are now reading.

We have to acknowledge that the current viability of our words is evidence of our success so far with the recalcitrant real, for von Glasersfeld's 'viable' does mean that we have a good chance of success with them, and that is repeated in our every moment of human life, but they remain 'Newtonian' for all that. We not only have no idea how much they miss, but we do know that they can *never* capture all that they claim to, although to get every statement under way we have to pretend that they do. It is a pity that the objectivists take the pretence for real. It could be said that, instead of conceding how much of the Fool there is in all of us, they are allowing themselves to be fooled by the real itself.

So there is risk in every identification. Yet, paradoxically, where is the risk for the 'you'? —*for 'you' is not going to die.* It is 'your' body, the humble animal, that will be dispersed into its elements, something that was only the avatar-soul's temporary lodging for the 'you'. Ironically, 'you' was put in it in the hope that what you say and do will help all future occupants of human bodies as players of the game to avoid suffering and find joy —which is the whole point of any sacrifice anyway, *whether it succeeds or not!* Tennyson, whose 'echoes roll from soul to soul' lines seem to be alone in capturing this novel view of immortality, could not help adding 'for ever and for ever' —the impossible hope (but perhaps not alone —the last verse of Edward Thomas's poem 'Adlestrop' could also be said to provide a metaphor for the endless diffusion of our meanings and hopes).

Bodies are helpless in the process — though they do help us to test the viability of the avatar-software which has been downloaded into us. One can't even say that bodies turn to us to look after them, though we have to, because that is the obvious but impossible aim of the whole social drama. They certainly won't rise on any Judgement Day, which is no more than part of the needful myth of a final justice, the final successful judging, or naming, of every*thing* that supposedly would have made all bodies safe forever. When St. Francis on his deathbed thanked 'his brother the ass', it has been suggested that by that he meant his body. We should copy St. Francis and look after our animal body as we do our dogs and our cats, a metaphorical performance in itself. There is no sense in saying you 'own' it no more than you own your cat or your dog. Like all the other possessions you claim to own, it is passed on after death 'for moth and rust to corrupt'. But what 'you' contribute to the great game will still go on as the influence of a past 'character' in that mutually imagined play — as it does now, which makes 'you' 'immortal' now for that influence cannot disappear however attenuated it becomes as long as people linked to you continue to be born. Isn't that what the religions have said? — that you have 'an immortal soul' *now*. By the end of 'your' life, the 'you', the empty, supposedly single, theoretical construct, *will have taken on real qualities from the body that it will carry back into the Game.* And the game itself, maintained by the living, has an imagined eternal quality, stretching back into the past and into the future. What your body helps you to do is not lost in history, for it should have 'played its part' with 'your' assistance, and *the 'you' could not have done* *it without the body*. And the satisfaction will be to know that you may be helping future bodies not yet born. All the rhythms and figurative concretenesses of language are owed to the gesturing and sounding body — Is not the very word 'language' from the Indo-European root 'dinghwa', meaning both *tongue* and *lick*? — the Latin 'lingua' and the English 'tongue' are both from this root.

However, it needs stressing what was urged above, that the body is *now* part of the blank real. It is not, as the Bible has it, that you were once 'dust' and, finally, it is 'unto dust thou shalt return': thou-as-a-body art dust already at this moment and have always been and always will be. One recalls Thomas Hardy's poem on some singing birds, 'Proud Songsters' in which he sees them as 'particles of grain,/ And earth, and air, and rain'. The fact that the body is a complicated result of evolution is irrelevant when its basis in the real is considered, and, in any case, 'you' had no hand in its formation. It is just a lucky bit of hardware that the social software working in the speakers around you as you grew up were able to invest with the YOU/I 'self'.

And so we won't think that it has all been no use because 'your' body is dead or because the time will come, with the Sun a red giant, when all bodies will be, for they always were 'dead'. Only then will the living game be over, the dream that creates and is created by human life leaving not a rack behind:

> till that doom is hurled
> That sears the ocean dry & wrecks the world.[6]

---

[6]   John Clare, 'Boston Church', ll. 27–8

In the science-fiction film *Knowing* (2009),[7] we are pre-sented with an end-of-the-world scenario much overlaid with Judaic biblical allusions. They include a final vision of a junior Adam and Eve in a Garden of Eden running through an idyllic harvest field towards a Tree of Knowl-edge, in addition to having escaped with angels' help, like Noah, a destruction of the world, in this case by fire, raised up like Elijah from the doomed Earth together with other favoured human beings. To its credit, though perhaps unconsciously in the psychoanalytic sense, the film wants to have it both ways: before the apocalyptic fire destroys the Earth, we see a last shot of the scientist hero of the film with his pastor father, and both are saying 'Everything will be fine.' For the Dawkinsian-atheist scientist this presumably means that he knows that his son will survive; for the pastor this means that God will unite them all in heaven after death. From the point of view of this book, neither interpre-tation applies: in the story the survival (on another planet) of the chosen is no more than a pleasant myth—the only justification of which is to see immortality presented in the sense described above, that is, as a continuation in the great Drama. However, it is clear that the script-writers meant us to take it literally. The old-religious father, on the other hand, can only accept immortality, fearfully, as a divine continuation of life. The film thus nicely presents the two points of view on immortality that the present theory regards as totally unacceptable.

Before leaving this film, there is a curious repetition of its conclusion in Peter Jackson's film *The Lovely Bones* (2010). The film ends with the ghost of a murdered girl, whom we

[7] Scriptwriters Ryne Douglas Pearson, Juliet Snowden and Stiles White, director Alex Proyas.

have followed throughout the film, advancing through an idyllic harvest field towards 'heaven', symbolized, it seems by the very same 'Tree of Knowledge' that appeared in the last shot of *Knowing*. Perhaps the CGI firm, having already created an inviting cornfield and a handsome tree, were economizing on software! What is also implied is that, as in the first film, there is a real heaven awaiting all of us. The Bible, it is worth recalling, associates in 'Genesis' the Serpent with the Tree of 'Knowledge', and makes it very clear that it is knowing that casts one *out of* the Garden of Eden.

Now we finally come to the point where we can turn the avatar-myth around; likenesses work in both directions. Jake Sully says, 'Everything is backwards now. Like out there is the true world, and in here is the dream.' The rules of language and behaviour that our family and society have instilled into us create this 'self'-conscious avatar within us, a downloading of software. But unlike the fate of actual software, the very software that created the 'self' has to perform it in a body, itself a part of the incalculable real that exists outside the counting, as I have just emphasized. In the film, the scientist Grace Augustine, recounting a tragic episode in her own experience as an avatar, says 'That kind of pain reaches back through the link'. The software was a hopeful set of rules, a theory, a 'dream' of what might be. Your laptop can't change its software—you can, and the task may be joyful or painful — for some of the downloading may over time become strongly entangled with the altered hardware, and, worse, tragically deep beyond a restart. We can't be brainwashed; if we were, the 'you' would disappear. Tragedy remains a real prospect for all of us, a dark conclusion that we all must confront. But the YOU cannot really become active until it is working in a body, no more than software can function outside the computer. This thought was one of the strengths of the story of Sam Tyler in the TV drama *Life on Mars* because its denouement showed Sam placing his moral commitment in the challenging life of 1973 and not the supposedly ideal one of 2006 — in this, matching Jake Sully's decision.

It is, of course, those who are alive at the moment who are playing the great game on the world's stage; they are the ones who, like those in a stadium briefly standing in a 'Mexican wave', have taken over the responsibility of keeping past 'souls' at work and the present ones in action. To quote John Cage: 'Theatre takes place all the time wherever one is, and art simply facilitates persuading one this is the case' (Cage, 1961, 174). So we can say that it is in a living world-wide-web of imagination that life at the moment is really going on, and we are trying to re-charge that web every time we speak. It excites me to think of this 'spirit' life going on all around me now, sparking electrically, for good or bad, in every word we say. The whole of a spider's web trembles if we but touch it with the tip of a finger. And this does not regard 'spirit' as anything occult or unreal.

And, as an ideal shimmering over the web, the world as a logical and mathematical structure is a 'pure', non-existent, imaginary creation that our faiths keep illumined just so that the chance of transformation may not be missed. I often think of how astronomers can identify a new planet (for example, Eris, a recently discovered 'Kuiper belt object' larger than Pluto: see the URL http://web.gps.caltech. edu/~mbrown/planetlila/). A number of photographs is taken of the same part of the sky at regular intervals; a computer is set to play these back in the form of a rapid slide-show; what becomes obvious is that one of the points of light moves across the field with all the rest remaining stationary — and is thus identifiable as the planet. In the same way, we can identify what perhaps needs transformation in our overall agreed system by first holding everything constant as already mutually known so that what is not mutually known becomes salient. This enacts the pattern of the Joke and the Story and the Statement.

One cannot ignore the fact that the body has to cope with the unintended, unexpected outcomes of the would-be digital rules, where every-'thing' has to be treated as if it *counts* for the same — and in the same way — for every-'one' else, *digit*ized on the fingers in the same manner for all, as the umpteen Commandments assume. Yet the word 'count' is significantly ambiguous: *to enumerate* and *to matter*. The body's distresses and delights bring up again and again the question of changing some rule, which is the reason why we talk, yet that rule is part of the system that constructed that 'self' and all the other ones in the first place. This is where the terrible challenge of sacrifice — and worse, the question of who is to accept the sacrifice — inevitably emerges. A 'self' may find itself comically or tragically divided, for the very desires and aversions that make it up have been directed from childhood by what has 'created' it and that software can't wholly be designed to anticipate all that the flows of thought and feeling it was directing in that body would do. Gregory Bateson's notion of the 'Double Bind' thus has application outside the context of mental disorder (Bateson, 1976, 6–7; see also Wright, 2008). Valuable thoughts are what *transform* 'knowledge' anyway, and their creativity cannot be foreseen. But that happens in games. The evil among us, like children (and some adults) who always want to win, are unwilling to play.

Eight

Incarnation as Avatarhood

These conclusions are clearly what the metaphor of the Incarnation—a putting of an imagined ideal into the *flesh*—was attempting to grasp. The early Christian church tried to face up to this with its notion of 'original sin', that we are all born being physically unable to match all the demands that 'self'-hood in a society may imply. Because the early church (and later ones), are superstitiously biased towards the pole of authority, the belief that the common taking-for-granted is the same for every-'body', it is impossible for them to accept that the 'sin' may be on the side of the software and not on that of a particular body or bodies. The software exists for the bodies anyway, and, if it doesn't work, it needs revision. To grasp the nettle—there may be an 'original sin' *on both sides*, for those who claim 'authority' and those who claim 'freedom'. Though an imagined god can be wholly good, there is no equating an objective 'God' with an objective 'Good'. This entails that there is such an 'original sin', not only in every 'self', but in every ethical 'system', like a mismatch in a scientific theory. Play, then, in the sense of *looseness*, as well as that of *pretence*, is present in the relation of the body to the social system, active in others (no wonder Mead emphasized play in the development of the child: Mead, 1934, 160).

The word 'sin' is usually taken to mean here an unexpected disparity between the ostensible aims of the software, its moral purposes, and its intended hardware, the body. But actual 'incarnation' is more like a metal seal being used on wax that contains unmelted lumps: if the pattern on the underside of the seal had been different, perhaps the lumps wouldn't have interfered with the print of the insignia — one could shift the blame about. But in either case, there is suffering for bodies, whether those at the centre of the social order or those at the periphery — or, again, perhaps, as in the tragic case, conflict and suffering for both (see *Oedipus Rex*).

After all, it is never denied that any moral system is ostensibly aiming at the final joy of all bodies (even though, in the Christian myth, some of them that don't match up to the sacred commandments will on Judgement Day be dispatched into eternal fire). The old-religious do not really want to acknowledge that tragedy can really occur; they say that it is all harmoniously resolved on that Judgement Day. Their unquestioning adherence to the system is a symptom of a blind, and certainly timid, sentimentality, instead of our 'adherence' to the faith-myth being, as it should be, *one that does not include belief.* They should observe Jake Sully, who becomes aware that he has rival purposes, under orders from Quaritch's society to destroy what he most values in the Na'vi one, of which he is now a member. Ironic that Quaritch, angry with Jake for changing sides, snarls, 'You forgot what team to play for', an unconscious admission that play is the all-embracing form, and play is incalculable. Within the play moral norms are created by us, and we have to take responsibility for them, especially when they do not produce what was expected.

Nine

The Acid Test for Faith

So we have an acid test by which we can check, not for faith as such, but at least for the circumstance most favourable for its being chosen by us as a guide for life. *If we hold all our identifications, including of our selves, as mutually imagined within the great myth-play of human life, then it is impossible to fall into superstition and believe the myths.* Play drives out superstition, the old-religious 'faiths', and enables you with courage, if not with certainty, to face the challenges that the real, without warning, can drop in front of you — this is what it is to have faith. It is to live bravely by poetic hypothesis, not in cowardly fashion by logical certainty. To quote Shakespeare's Touchstone again, 'for the truest poetry is the most feigning' (*As You Like It*, III, iii, 16–17). You will, inescapably, know that sacrifice could await you. Play in the myths, not pray, if you want your life to have meaning, and thus you will change the myths. Now when people say to you 'Language is what makes us human' (and language is full of myth), you can add that without this kind of faith when you speak you are not rising to the really human level, the happiest and safest one — though, in the words of the witches to Banquo, there will be times when 'you are not so happy' as others but yet 'much happier', namely, when you are accepting sacrifice. It is important to see that this cannot be a slavish, automatic self-sacrifice: there is no more a pure altruism than there is a pure selfishness; each danger-fraught occasion will demand its own 'painful-for-some-one' resolution. To think otherwise is to be back with the notion that the 'original sin' can only ever be the body's and never the system's.

What this necessarily implies, of course, is that the old-religious were actually inside the play *without knowing that they were*, which places them in the same trap as the poet John Clare when in July 1830 his madness began to show itself: while watching a performance of *The Merchant of Venice* at a Peterborough theatre, he jumped up from his seat when Portia accused Shylock and shouted 'You villain! You murderous villain!' He was not playing. If you don't want to fall into his mistake of literally believing that there are 'blue devils' (and gods), you must make-believe, with your eyes, and the eyes of all those about you — also making-believe — open. Otherwise, you are being superstitious. James Cameron, in his script for *Avatar*, in the scene of the attack on the great tree, directs the actress taking Mo'at, the clan's wise woman, at the moment she cuts the supposed enemy's, Jake's, bonds, to show '*faith*' as well as 'horror' in her eyes.

Ten

We are all Avatars

So, after our winding walk through the wood, we have again reached the myths of the holy avatars, Krishna and Christ. They have been construed altogether too much by the superstitious as their representing an authority beyond question, personifications of 'the Good', beings that will put everything right for the timid. It is true that there have been Christian theologians who could not help but interpret the Crucifixion as symbolizing the inevitability of sacrifice and of the sinless god 'suffering for our sins', but they could not bring themselves to read the Crucifixion *as showing the god being punished for its own 'sin' of demanding with its current rules too much from bodies.* Whenever we speak, we are implying that we are trying to put some existing 'rule' right. Consider the Birdwatchers.

This is something that has not been said before: the old-religious do not want to let it out that the existing 'authorities' have no monopoly on authority. The very word 'authorities', nicely pluralized, is an attempt to fix authority on those in power — via a shaky metonym, to suggest that the 'authorities' actually have the ideal Authority.[1] A pure Authority, after all, does not know the way to

---

[1]   Compare the metonym 'a beauty' for a beautiful woman, where the abstract noun is used for the thing possessing it — similarly, 'my love' for the person loved.

heaven: it only plays that it does. The 'authorities' do not want to let it out that moral choice is much more a democratic matter than has been admitted. Moral life goes on in the daily challenges of our incarnation, not in the bodiless idealizing of morality. In their view the 'common people' are not to be *trusted*: anarchy may result if they knew what religion really was—namely, an imagined, mutually maintained drama in progress. Notice that, significantly, this distrust is a withholding of faith. They want the common people to trust them, but they do not trust the people in return, not until history forces them to. Those who suspect this theory fear that 'the common people', told that all objectivity is a fiction sustained by faith, will mock such an eccentric guide for life; better that they should be kept in quiet superstitious subjection by literalizing the religious myths (there are several religious thinkers who adopt this view: see Wright, 2005, 210). Nevertheless, the objection is weak: the anthropologist Robert Marett reminded us that 'the savage is a good actor' (Marett, 1914, 45)—why then not the common people? The savage played his myths, as we should. Play is at the origin of language, and thus of the human (Wright, 2009). The supposed distaste for poetry in popular culture is performatively denied in every other pop lyric, every new pop-idiom.

What goes on in democratic parliaments is definitely much nearer to the character of moral dilemmas than has been noticed, and the reason is the same: there the (hopeful) negotiation goes on to effect the 'best' outcome. Both parliamentarians and moralists of both left and right should realize that a 'best outcome' may not be achievable without painful sacrifice from both sides of the chamber. Even more so in the stubborn confrontations of the world (Israeli/

Palestinian, Sri Lankan/Tamil, Balkan Christian/Balkan Muslim, Turk/Kurd, Slovak/Roma, etc., etc.). To alter the script while we are playing is not easy, but it is easier if those in conflict know that they are inside the structure of a play. Otherwise, the 'opposition' is not a 'loyal opposition', nor even is the 'government' loyal.

The film *Avatar* shows the incarnated Jake Sully rejecting the rules of his own avatarhood, and this is no surprise since the chance of history over the past six hundred years or so has shown a greater and greater resistance to the older politico-religious hierarchical systems. We have so much of that history within us, we can hardly help cheering Jake Sully on when he cries 'Freedom!' In the 21st century we have reached the stage where it appears incumbent upon all political leaders, such as Bush and Blair in the Iraq War, to mouth 'Freedom!' as their slogan, a sad indication, not that we have forgotten what authority is, but forgotten the fact that one cannot have one without the other. It makes as much sense to cry 'Authority!', to paint 'Authority' on our banners—but, admit it, reader, doesn't our 600-year upbringing make that sound absurd? Yet it is in the interlocking of authority and freedom where the splendours and miseries of our history take place. Sacrifices have been, are being and will be made for both.

We can no longer automatically put the 'individual' first—each 'individual' is already 'divided'. *Cogito, ergo sum*, 'I think; therefore I am', is a pathetically misleading motto—unless we redefine 'think' to acknowledge its intersubjective, transformatory, non-egoistic nature. There is no such thing as a pure ego. But it is equally misleading to think that a 'social cohesion', in which we all march the same way like a military parade in Rangoon or Pyongyang,

provides an instant solution. How cowardly such parades
are! It is what makes them so comic — their perfect obedi-
ence, evidenced in their goose-stepping over-exertion,
supposedly acknowledging a perfect and non-existent
authority (think of all those poor bodies being forcibly put
through such nonsense!). What is derivable from this
thought, of course, is the origin of the totalitarian demands
that were reflected in the films, of the fascist myth-believer
Colonel Quaritch and his ilk, and all those outside drama
who parade themselves as 'leaders of the nation'. In faith,
we all know well that we are not all marching the same way,
though we have to play at doing so. Encouraging to note
that speech does take place with some success, which is
evidence of the worth of play, but not of perfect success in
referring!

Perhaps we should always think that we are winking to
each other when we speak (taking Lear's Fool or Groucho
Marx as our exemplars) — and, in addition, think we are
winking to each other when we, with immense seriousness,
bow before our symbolic 'monarch' (*'single ruler'*) — in Brit-
ain, our Queen. We do need such symbolic rulers — well
away from the 'prime ministers' and 'presidents', just as we
need symbolic gods — for the *powerless* Kings and Queens
and gods represent the hoped-for unity, the fantasy that we
can never achieve but which is helpful *to play*. What we
don't want is that the theatrical aura of that fantasy, a poetic
symbol of our impossible faith, should settle round Adolf
Hitlers or Idi Amins or Pol Pots or Than Shwes or Kim Jong
Ils, all of whom claim a godlike faultless authority for their
actual power, and thus busy themselves imprisoning,
torturing or killing anyone who disagrees with their purest
of wishes for the 'nation' — wishing to enforce a demonic

'possession' on all they control in their would-be *Matrix* world. It is significant that they should wish to torture and kill for that is an unconscious admission that it is from the body that challenges to their current 'rule' begin. One can quote Confucius (whose biopic, recall, is at present the enforced replacement for *Avatar* on Chinese 2D screens): 'It is just that I so detest inflexibility' (Confucius, 1979 [ca. 490 B.C.], 129). Similarly with those who place themselves at the Body pole, the anarchists, for their rejection of control in the name of 'freedom' is equally pure in its terrorist demands, equally pathological in its rush to assassinate. Extremes meet in the refusal of both poles to compromise 'their' will. Neither can accept the 'splitting' pain of incarnation, within which there is no 'single' will. The French psychoanalyst Jacques Lacan drew attention to the inevitability of the supposedly conscious subject being 'split' (Lacan, 1977, 285).

In the film, a better world was arrived at in the past for the Na'vi, their clans having been 'brought together' after 'a time of great sorrow': for us the twentieth-century and the opening of the twenty-first has certainly been that. Perhaps a better world will await us if we can face up to what our avatarhood, our incarnation, really is—an inescapable 'self'-division. Will it not also help those opponents locked in intractable conflicts to know that it is normal for such conflicts sometimes to occur, that the behaviour of the 'enemy' is not solely motivated by mindless hate, thus perhaps enabling the participants to shift toward mutually sacrificial resolutions? Would this not be a 'loving of one's enemy'?

So we are all avatars, all incarnated within language that made us, interpreting the rules of our human being our own way. Although we in faith must try to behave, in the meaning of every word, as if we were not interpreting them 'our own way', as if we all have the avatar-god as 'guardian angel' inside our 'selves' to guide us, we have to accept that the transforming irony that is the energy of all stories places us in a story now, where human desire struggles with human desire without, necessarily, a final denouement. Those who do actively believe that they have God's voice inside to guide them are the ones 'possessed by the Devil'. But what new ways have we to live in order to keep the game fair?

We can use the clue that avatars are now turning up in our popular culture, whether it is in film, literature and drama, or such web activities as *Second Life*. This is an unconscious acknowledgement of their moral and philosophical significance. We need to bring *imagination* back into our lives after its dismissal by both secular and religious pressures. The Chinese were wise enough in the past to use actors to enhance their sacred ceremonies. This is itself a reminder that imagination is there in our lives already, in every statement we make, as our only final, *unachievable* purpose. John Cage was right: art 'facilitates' the play. We need the wonder of *play* in our communities, a wonder that perhaps could create cathedrals and dramas and poems and paintings and dances and songs in our mundane world—even take back the old cathedrals again, and the holy paintings and the holy music!—Whose are they anyway?

If Thomas Hardy could have read this theory, one might have put it to him that a hope he tentatively expressed has been realized. In the 'Apology' with which he prefaced his book of poems *Late Lyrics and Earlier* (1922) he concluded with this thought:

> It may be a forlorn hope, a mere dream, that of an alliance
> between religion, which must be retained unless the world
> is to perish, and complete rationality, which must come,
> unless also the world is to perish, by means of the interfus-
> ing effect of poetry (Hardy, 1952, 525)

We can take 'complete rationality' to be the imagined coincidence of all our perspectives on the real, and 'religion' to
be the courageous faith that is demanded of us by the inescapable predicament that travelling with others between
birth and death through the real involves, namely, the one
that arises out of the realization that there is no such coincidence. It is fear and the distrust it creates that prevents people seeing that 'rationality', 'objectivity', and 'truth' to
which they cling *indeed have to be clung to but only as an imagined convergence of our wishes* — otherwise we could never
speak (look again at how the Birdwatchers, together, *spoke*).
It may be claimed that this theory, whether or not it has succeeded, has attempted to bring about, as Hardy wished, a
paradoxical 'alliance' by means of the poetic, of the
'interfusings', the transformations of play-as-faith — after
all, you cannot transform unless you both started out with a
pretended perfect agreement, the essential pretence of any
kind of play, the one that is fooling none of those sharing the
game.

There is no doubt that music must not be forgotten. Our
humble bodies love the transformations of rhythm — were
not brains evolved to learn, that is endlessly update old
interpretations? — *which is what a rhythm does with every beat,
again and again making the familiar novel.* No wonder music is
the queen of the arts. I was greatly cheered up today on
seeing in the supermarket a little girl of three or so *skipping*
after her mother. Professor Nina Kraus of Northwestern
University at this year's (2010) meeting of the American

Association for the Advancement of Science has been able to show that teaching children to play a musical instrument produced marked improvements in speech and general development. One has to mention here the amazing achievement of Yutaka Sugino in Sapporo in Japan who has brought music in the Hokkaido International School to an extraordinary level of performance. For over ten years he has regularly drawn in a large number of students, a good third or more of the school, in grand musical performances which evidence remarkable variety of styles, tribal to cathedral. One might instance alone one's realization as one listens that they are all singing closely and confidently *in tune*, at the same time as joining in a precise and expressive choreography of gesture and dance. And 'Hip hip hooray!' (a rhythmic shout) for Gareth Malone! — he who, in England, has brought music to music-less schools and, against all expectations, created a hugely enthusiastic choir in South Oxhey in Hertfordshire (see his website below).[2] That choir's concert was definitely not a Nuremburg rally.[3] Some of the critics of *Avatar*, probably unconsciously fearing that kind of fascist handling of myth, mocked the film for showing the Na'vi in a public dance ritual—which betrays in those critics a misguided suspicion, Enlightenment-inspired, of myth-as-played.

One can, without becoming a superstitious New-Age fanatic, even celebrate 'Gaia' or 'Eywa' thus—even 'God'. Let us all behave as if there is a faith-god or gods—after all, that is what the old-religious *are really trying to do anyway now without knowing it* as they go into their cathedrals and

---

[2]   http://www.garethmalone.com/
[3]   Hitler gave myth a bad name it does not deserve, because he was superstitious—he believed his fantasies.

temples and mosques and synagogues, and sing their hymns! We do it happily with Santa Claus, and consequently enjoy the myth of worldwide, generous, familial love. The kill-joys who mock Santa Claus are Christmas versions of Dawkins. Nor is there anything to stop us joining in the religious celebrations of other religions, such as the Hindu Diwali or the Jewish Hannukah, their 'festivals of light', or the Muslim Eid Ul Adha, the Day of Happiness and Reconciliation. None of this would be superstition, for the superstitious *believe* the myth. Furthermore, it would help the superstitious to divest themselves of their fear.

Luckily, the world is still enchantable by imagination: you can start with 'the meanest flower that blows'. But, Pope Benedict, that doesn't make us pantheists, or New-Age tree-huggers, for *we don't believe a word of it!* — which is easy, seeing that is what sensible children, who know how to play, do already. Knowing how to play also implies knowing how to change the rules by doing so, that is, if one can. So this is not exactly atheism, though it is a materialist who propounds it: let us call it 'faitheism'.

Follow Shelley's advice:

Hope till hope creates
From its own wreck the thing it contemplates.

— otherwise Pandora will let out even more of the woes of the world.

References

Austin, John L. (1970) 'A plea for excuses'. In *Philosophical Papers*, J.O. Urmson and G.J. Warnock (eds.) (Oxford: Oxford University Press).

Bateson, Gregory (1976) 'Toward a theory of schizophrenia,' in *Double Bind: The Foundation of the Communicational Approach to the Family.* Carlos E. Sluzki and Donald C. Ransom (eds.) (New York: Grune and Stratton), pp. 3-32.

Brandom, Robert B. (1994) *Making it Explicit: Reasoning, Representing, and Discursive Commitment* (Cambridge, Massachusetts: Harvard University Press).

Cage, John (1973) *Silence: Lectures and Writings* (Indianapolis, IN: Wesleyan Paperback).

Confucius (1974 [ca. 490 B.C.]) *The Analects.* D. C. Lau (trans. and ed.) (Harmondsworth: Penguin Books).

Dawkins, Richard (2006) *The God Delusion* (London: Transworld Publishers).

Dennett, Daniel (1983) 'Reflections (on David H. Sanford's "Where was I?")', in Douglas R. Hofstadter and Daniel C. Dennett (eds.), *The Mind's Eye: Fantasies ans Reflections on Self and Soul* (Harmondsworth: Penguin Books), pp. 240-1.

Dennett, Daniel (2006) *Breaking the Spell: Religion as a Natural Phenomenon* (London: Allen Lane).

Dilthey, Wilhelm (1913-67) *Gesammelte Schriften.* 14 vols. (Göttingen: Vandenhoeck & Ruprecht).

Eagleton, Terry (2010) *On Evil* (New Haven and London: Yale University Press).

Evans, Gareth (1982) *The Varieties of Reference.* John McDowell (ed.) (Oxford: Clarendon Press).

Feinberg, Joel (1964) 'Action and responsibility', in *Philosophy in America*, Max Black (ed.) (London: Allen and Unwin), pp. 134-60.

Glasersfeld, Ernst von (1984) 'An Introduction to Radical Constructivism', in Paul Watzlawick, (ed.), The *Invented Reality* (New York NY: W. W. Norton), pp. 17-40.

Gleiser, Marcelo (2010) 'Perfectly imperfect', *New Scientist*, Vol. 206, No. 2759. 28–9.

Gregory, R.L (1993) 'Hypothesis and Illusion: Explorations in perception and science,' in Edmond Wright (ed.), *New Representationalisms: Essays in the Philosophy of Perception* (Aldershot: Ashgate).

Hampshire, Stuart (1970) *Thought and Action* (London: Chatto and Windus).

Harman, Gilbert (1990) 'The Intrinsic Quality of Experience', in *Philosophical Perspectives, 4, Action Theory and Philosophy of Mind,* J. Tomberlin (ed.) (Atascadero, California: Ridgeview Publishing Company), pp. 31-52.

Hitchens, Christopher (2008) *God is not Great: How Religion Poisons Everything* (London: Atlantic Books).

Joyce, James (1947) *Ulysses*. London: John Lane, The Bodley Head.

Lacan, Jacques (1977) *Écrits; a Selection*. Alan Sheridan (trans.) (London: Tavistock Publications Limited).

Lowe, E.J. and Rami, A. (2009) *Truth and Truth-Making* (Stocksfield: Acumen).

McDowell, John (1994) *Mind and World* (Cambridge, MA: Harvard University Press).

Marett, R.R. (1914) *The Threshold of Religion* (London: Methuen).

Mead, George Herbert (1934) *Mind, Self, and Society*, C.W. Morris (ed.) (Chicago: Chicago University Press).

Onfray, Michel (2007) *In Defence of Atheism: The Case against Christianity, Judaism and Islam* (London: Serpent's Tail).

Plotinus (1934 [ca. 253]) *The Essence of Plotinus*, (Grace H. Turnbull (ed.). Stephen McKenna (trans.) (New York: Oxford University Press).

Rommetveit, Ragnar (1974) *On Message Structure: A Framework for the Study of Language and Communication* (London: John Wiley & Sons).

Royce, Josiah (1976 [1899]) *The World and the Individual*, 2 vols. (Gloucester MA: Peter Smith).

Ryle, Gilbert (1949) *The Concept of Mind* (Harmondsworth: Penguin Books).

Ryle, Gilbert (1971) 'The theory of meaning', in *Collected Papers*, Vol. II. (London: Hutchinson), pp. 350-72.

Schutz, Alfred (1962) *Collected Papers, Vol. I: The Problem of Social Reality* (The Hague: Martinus Nijhoff).

Steiner, George (1998) *After Babel: Aspects of Language and Translation* (Oxford and New York: Oxford University Press).

Vaihinger, Hans (1924) *The Philosophy of 'As If'* (London: Kegan Paul, Trench, Trübner and Co).

Wiggins, David (1986) 'On Singling out an Object Determinately', in Philip Pettit and John McDowell (eds.), *Subject, Thought and Context* (Oxford, Clarendon Press), pp. 169-80.

Wittgenstein, Ludwig (1967 [1953]) *Philosophical Investigations.* G.E.M. Anscombe (trans.) (Oxford: Basil Blackwell).

Wright, Edmond (1978) 'Sociology and the Irony Model', *Sociology*, 12, 523–43.

Wright, Edmond (1990) 'New Representationalism', *Journal for the Theory of Social Behaviour*, 20: 65–92.

Wright, Edmond (1996) 'What it isn't like', *American Philosophical Quarterly*, 23, No. 1, 23–45.

Wright, Edmond (2005) *Narrative, Perception, Language, and Faith* (Basingstoke: Palgrave Macmillan).

Wright, Edmond, ed. (2008) *The Case for Qualia* (Cambridge MA: MIT Press).

Wright, Edmond (2009) 'Gregory Bateson: epistemology, language, play and the Double Bind', *Anthropoetics – The Journal of Generative Anthropology*, Volume ISSN1083XIV, number 1 (Summer 2008), http://www.anthropoetics.ucla.edu/ap1401/

Index